T0060157

CHICKEN SOUP FOR THE CHOCOLATE LOVER'S SOUL

Chicken Soup for the Chocolate Lover's Soul
Indulging in Our Sweetest Moments
Jack Canfield, Mark Victor Hansen, Patricia Lorenz

Published by Backlist, LLC,
a unit of Chicken Soup for the Soul Publishing, LLC. www.chickensoup.com

Copyright ©2012 by Chicken Soup for the Soul Publishing, LLC. All Rights Reserved.
No part of this publication may be reproduced, stored in a retrieval system or transmitted in any form or by any means, electronic, mechanical, photocopying, recording or otherwise, without the written permission of the publisher.

CSS, Chicken Soup for the Soul, and its Logo and Marks are trademarks of Chicken Soup for the Soul Publishing LLC.

Cover design by Larissa Hise Henoch
Originally published in 2007 by Health Communications, Inc.

Distributed to the booktrade by Simon & Schuster. SAN: 200-2442

Publisher's Cataloging-in-Publication Data
(Prepared by The Donohue Group)

Chicken soup for the chocolate lover's soul : indulging in our sweetest moments / [compiled by] Jack Canfield, Mark Victor Hansen, [and] Patricia Lorenz.

  p. : ill. ; cm.

  Originally published: Deerfield Beach, FL : Health Communications, c2007.
  ISBN: 978-1-62361-066-1

  1. Chocolate--Anecdotes. 2. Anecdotes. I. Canfield, Jack, 1944- II. Hansen, Mark Victor. III. Lorenz, Patricia.

TX415 .C42 2012
394.1/2   2012944777

PRINTED IN THE UNITED STATES OF AMERICA
on acid free paper

22 21 20 19 18 17 16 15 14 13   01 02 03 04 05 06 07 08 09 10

CHICKEN SOUP FOR THE CHOCOLATE LOVER'S SOUL

Indulging in Our Sweetest Moments

Jack Canfield
Mark Victor Hansen
Patricia Lorenz

Backlist, LLC, a unit of
Chicken Soup for the Soul Publishing, LLC
Cos Cob, CT
www.chickensoup.com

Contents

2. TICKLING THE TASTE BUDS

3. RELAXING RENDEZVOUS

Contents

Introduction

Chocolate is a word that conjures up a plethora of feelings, tastes, smells, sights, memories, cravings, and pleasures.

Chocolate is the stuff of mood-lifting happiness. It lands on our tongues, melts slowly into a rich, creamy, sweet taste that soothes our taste buds and somehow makes us feel better than we did before it touched our lips.

From the moment our mothers or grandfathers or favorite aunts or babysitters mix a little chocolate syrup into milk when we're toddlers, we're hooked. Chocolate milk becomes the favorite drink of childhood, followed by chocolate candies, candy bars, ice cream, brownies, puddings, pies, and cakes. It's practically addictive, this rich, dreamy, creamy mixture, not physically addictive, but mentally. We want it. We really, really want it.

Before we know it, we're either selling chocolate thin mint cookies or we're buying them, squirreling them away and devouring them like popcorn. Then comes Halloween, when our children collect bags and bags of candy, but treasure mostly the little chocolate candy bars. And, of course, it's only the chocolate that Mom sneaks out of those bags on a daily basis until thoughts of Thanksgiving and Christmas take over. Then new forms of chocolate emerge on the scene in the shape of trees, bells, stars, and oozing white stuff surrounding cherries covered in milk chocolate.

As adults our chocolate tastes become more sophisticated. Chocolate liquor. Truffles. Chocolate coffees. Mocha everything: desserts, ice creams, party drinks. We travel and buy chocolate in other countries and compare. German. Swiss. Italian. Spanish. French. We come home and fill our chocolate spaces with bonbons, bars, truffles, and dark, dark chocolate with real bean pieces inside, because evidence supports the fact that dark chocolate is actually good for us.

For women, chocolate becomes the drug of choice to get us through our crabby, crampy periods, pregnancy cravings, and finally pre-, during-, and post-menopausal hot flash days when only chocolate seems like our best friend. Chocolate heals, soothes, enlightens, and just makes us feel good.

We plan sophisticated parties around chocolate, from bridal showers to receptions, birthdays, office parties, and hen fests. We discover the chocolate fountain, with fruits, cakes, marshmallows, and Rice Krispies treats finding their way to the end of the fondue stick where we dip it into luscious chocolate sauce. It drips on our chins, lies on our lips, tickles our tongues, and tantalizes our taste buds before we swallow. Then we want more. Much more.

No matter where we are—the corner grocery, gas station, drugstore, mall, specialty shops on Main Street, USA, or Fifth Avenue in New York—we spot chocolate everywhere. We slow down, lick our lips, and give in to the hundreds of shapes, sizes, flavors, and passions of chocolate. We linger at the chocolate chip cookie store in the mall, aching for an entire bag of warm chocolate chip mini-cookies but settle for two of the big ones.

We all have our favorites. Creamy chocolate bars. Fudge. Nonpareils. Brownies. Six-layer chocolate cake laced with caramel and cream frostings. Chocolate turtle cheese cake. Malted milk balls. Ice cream swirled with chocolate ribbons and topped with hot fudge. Chocolate confections shipped in from all over the globe. Warm chocolate pudding with whipped cream on top. Kisses. Hugs. Heart-shaped boxes.

Chocolate is one of those pleasures in life that's relatively inexpensive, easy to obtain, makes us feel a little better physically and mentally, and if we don't overdo it, can be good for us, according to some recent studies.

Chocolate is more than a food, more than a treat. It's a passion, a must-have. Sometimes it's a simple pleasure that can help soothe the most complicated day. For most of us, women especially, chocolate isn't a want. It's a need.

Sometimes our chocolate cravings leave us feeling guilty. As you read these true stories and experiences from people of all ages, races, and backgrounds, my hope is that with each melt-in-your-mouth bite of your favorite chocolate treat, you'll take comfort in knowing that the majority of humans enjoy and treasure their chocolate cravings as much as you do. One thing I know: life is too short to live it without chocolate.

Patricia Lorenz

1

DELECTABLE DELIGHTS

Fifteen-Cent Surprise

You're on my list of things I love most—
right below chocolate.

Mary Englund Murphy

I t was December 1963. Jack and I wanted to give each other something special on our first Christmas together, but we had no extra money for gifts. We had dated, fallen in love, and married all in the span of three months. We were young, in love, and broke—flat broke.

Jack was a private in the Marine Corps. He was stationed at the Naval Weapons Station, Charleston, South Carolina. The nicest house we could afford on Jack's ninety-dollar-a-month salary was half of a rickety old duplex. It sat smack-dab in the middle of a cow pasture on the backside of Goose Creek. It was drafty, the roof leaked, and it had no hot water. But we were together, and that was what mattered most to us.

Unknown to me, as December rolled along, Jack was determined to surprise me with something on our first Christmas together. On December 19, he hid a small hatchet under his field jacket. He slid his hands into his work gloves, pulled his cap down to keep his ears warm, and took a moonlit stroll to the back side of the cow pasture. About an hour later he returned with a pathetic little pine tree and a huge grin. That little tree's scrawny branches spread out like angel's wings to me. I welcomed the surprise with childish delight.

"Here's an empty coffee can, Jack. We can stand the tree in it," I said. Jack filled the coffee can with South Carolina clay and jammed the tree's tiny trunk into it. I draped one of my scarves around the can. Then I decorated the pitiful tree with my earrings, necklaces, and bracelets. The rhinestones glittered like tinsel. "It's not the biggest tree in the world, but it's the most beautiful Christmas tree I've ever had," I said as I planted a kiss on Jack's cheek. I leaned on his strong shoulder and sighed with happiness.

But Jack wasn't satisfied. He wanted a gift to place under that tree. On Christmas Eve he stopped at the PX on his way home from duty. He had a grand total of twenty-one cents in his pocket. For an hour he walked up and down the aisles searching for something—anything— he could buy for the love of his life with such meager savings. He had almost given up when his eyes locked on to a small sign that read "15¢." He grabbed one, paid for it, and headed home with his treasure tucked inside the pocket of his field jacket.

That night Jack and I ate bologna sandwiches in front of our Christmas tree. We sang Christmas carols and snuggled near the gas space heater. Around midnight Jack disappeared into the bedroom. He reappeared with his right hand hidden behind his back. His mouth went dry and his hands shook as he announced, "Close your eyes now. It's a surprise."

"Oh, Jack, you shouldn't have spent money on a gift. We can't afford it."

"I couldn't let Christmas come and go without doing something special for the most beautiful girl in the world. Close your eyes, and hold out your hand."

I must admit I was excited. I giggled like a kid. Jack placed his treasure in my open palm. "I know it isn't much. But, well, it's your favorite and you're *my* favorite." He exhaled loudly. "Merry Christmas!"

I opened my eyes. Resting in my palm was a miniature box containing four chocolate-covered confections. I pulled the little treasure close to my heart, then wrapped both arms around my hero's neck.

"This is the most wonderful gift I've ever received. It's so good to be loved by you, Jack. I can't believe that you're all mine. You're the best thing about my life."

In the years that followed, our finances improved. Each Christmas the trees got fancier. Each year the presents got bigger and more expensive. But for thirty-four Christmases one gift occupied a place of honor under our Christmas tree. Every year until his death, Jack gave me his love—wrapped in a box of chocolate. And every year he became more and more my hero.

Jean Tomlinson
As told to Jean Matthew Hall

Skinny Dotty and Her Chocolates

All I really need is love, but a little chocolate now and then doesn't hurt!

Lucy Van Pelt
Peanuts, Charles M. Schulz

I live in a co-op apartment in Chelsea, New York City. It's like a small town here—our own little community. There's a family feeling, complete with gossip and tiffs and warm hugs and belly laughs. Skinny Dotty is a fixture. One time I asked if I could paint her portrait. She said, "Maybe if I were younger and didn't have so many wrinkles. But it's too late now." I asked her how old she was, and she wagged her finger back and forth and said, "I'll never tell." I'm left to guess she's seventy-five.

Dotty is shaped like a pencil, her blond hair in a bob where the eraser would be. She loves to wear clothes with pictures of cats on them—baseball caps with cats, T-shirts with cats, sneakers with cats, socks with cats, purses with cats.

Dotty spends most of her time checking on other people's cats and watering plants in the neighbors' apartments. I see her in the lobby, on the elevator, or when I pass through our private garden. Every time I see Dotty, she insists on giving me chocolate, handfuls of it. I try to refuse, worried about my dental bills and my waistline, but she ignores me and puts gobs of the little chocolates right into my pockets. Because I've tried to refuse, my guilt is gone. I eat each one, slowly, ecstatically, savoring every rich, creamy bite.

The superintendent's office is a cubicle right off the lobby entrance. It has a window that faces the lobby. A million years ago, Dotty placed a glass bowl on the ledge of the window and she fills it with chocolates every single day. I've witnessed the mailman grab whole handfuls and push them deep into his pockets. He thinks I don't see him.

Violet, a cranky, stout fiftyish woman who kvetches loudly at every annual shareholder meeting, regularly swipes more than her share. When she stands next to skinny Dotty, they look like the number ten. When Violet corners me in the lobby and I make the mistake of asking, "How are you?" she responds with her litany of complaints.

Violet snatches handfuls of the chocolates, snaps her fake snakeskin purse open, drops the chocolates in, *plink, plink, plunk,* then she snaps the purse shut. She doesn't even care that I see her. If I were to ask why she took so many, I'm sure she'd say, "Because nobody knows how I suffer."

Violet doesn't tip the staff at Christmas. Dotty tips them and makes them cookies, even though she can't possibly be wealthy. Her husband was ill and out of work for a very long time. He would sit in the garden in his wheelchair with a book on his lap, snoring. Dotty often came downstairs and put a blanket over his legs while he snoozed. He reminded me of a beat-up old lawn chair. One night

Jimmy died in his sleep. That week when I ran into Dotty in the lobby, she looked disoriented.

I asked, "What's wrong?"

"Jimmy died," she said.

"I'm so sorry to hear," I said. "You must miss him terribly."

"Yes, the apartment is so quiet now." Her voice trailed off and she looked down at her sneakers with the cats on them. Then, as if someone changed the channel, she perked up and said, "Want some chocolates?"

I wanted to say something about Jimmy, about her pain, but instead I responded to her question, "Oh, no, you keep them for yourself."

As usual, she ignored me and stuffed a handful into my jacket pocket. As soon as I got to the elevator, I popped one into my mouth. The chocolate felt warm and snuggly and melted over my tongue. I felt a slight elevation in my mood. I slowly unwrapped the next one. I listened to the tin foil crinkle as I whiffed that spellbinding smell. Pop, it went into my mouth. By the time I got to my apartment on the third floor, all five chocolates had disappeared down the hatch and my day had improved 100 percent.

I often saw Dotty heading over to fill the glass bowl with a red and white bag from CVS drugstore. One day while I was at CVS, I walked over to the candy aisle and was surprised by how much those bags of chocolates cost. I suddenly felt bad for skinny Dotty always worrying about everybody else's chocolate cravings. I decided to surprise her and buy chocolates for her. I stocked my cart with Hershey's Kisses, mini-Snickers, Milk Duds, and Reese's Pieces.

I headed back to the building. I entered through the back gate that opens to the garden, and sure enough, there was Dotty, as usual, chatting with a neighbor on a bench. I ran up to Dotty with a wide, proud grin.

"These are for you, my dear!" I exclaimed as I handed over the stuffed plastic bag.

"Oh, what's this? Aren't you sweet," she said, smiling. But when she opened the bag her eyebrows twisted and her smile withered.

"What's wrong?" I said.

"I don't like chocolate," she said.

"But, but . . ." I sputtered, "then why do you always buy it for everybody?"

"So people will smile at me," she said, very matter-of-factly.

I felt embarrassed, as if she were standing there naked. I wanted to cover her up. I wanted to drape a shawl around her bony shoulders. I wanted to fold her little pencil frame and stick her on my lap. It was all I could do not to burst out crying.

I breathed in deeply and summoned my composure. I gave her a gigantic hug and told her how lucky we all are to have her looking after us. Skinny Dotty beamed and handed me back the big bag of chocolates. I walked over to the glass bowl on the ledge and filled it up to the top.

Dorri Olds

Cards and Kisses

I believe there's biblical evidence that
confirms there will be chocolate in heaven.
Revelation 7:17 says there will be no more
tears. That pretty much cinches it for me.

Rhonda Rhea

I t was Valentine's Day, and we were broke. It wasn't uncommon for us to be low on funds. Raising three kids on a pastor's salary often left us with "too much month at the end of the money." My husband, Bruce, complained, "You're my valentine and I don't have anything for you on Valentine's Day. I don't have money for flowers, much less jewelry."

Trying to comfort him, I explained, "You don't have to get me expensive stuff. We try to teach the folks at church not to go into debt when a heartfelt card is more than enough." Bruce took my heartfelt card idea to heart.

That afternoon I stopped by the church office after picking the kids up from school. Bruce waved me into his office and presented me with a bright red envelope and a small bag of Hershey's Kisses before he headed downstairs to a meeting. Opening the card, I found myself lost in the words and the images as tears welled up in my eyes.

The secretary called to me from the outer office, bringing me back to reality, "I have some questions about brochures for the upcoming women's event. Can you help me?" she asked. I laid the card down on my husband's desk and yelled back, "I'll be right there."

I wasn't gone for more than twenty minutes, but when I returned, I found my oldest daughter, Sarah, curled up like a cat in her dad's wingback chair, cradling the card carefully in her lap and polishing off what little was left of the Hershey's Kisses. "This card is beautiful, Mom," she cooed, stroking it with her sticky, chocolate-covered fingers. "Who gave it to you?"

"Well, I hope Daddy did, considering what it says." I chuckled.

"It's the most awesome card I've ever seen," she responded, batting her big blue eyes as only a thirteen-year-old girl with a headful of romantic notions could do. Just then my husband walked through his office door. Grabbing him around the neck I planted a big kiss—one on each cheek. "Wow, what was that for?"

"The first kiss was for my beautiful card; the second one was for teaching our daughter by example to choose a man who will love and cherish her," I whispered in his ear.

"I need to give you more cards," Bruce smiled.

"And chocolate," I quipped as we all gathered up my things to head home. I kept the card out on the kitchen counter to enjoy for a while before I tucked it into my keepsake drawer to remember forever.

Eight Valentine's Days passed and that beautiful blue-eyed thirteen-year-old was now a blushing bride. I opened my keepsake drawer, looking for grandma's jewelry to offer her something old to go with the something new and borrowed to round out her wedding repertoire. There next to grandma's pearls was the Valentine's Day card—complete with chocolate fingerprints.

The experts are right: values are caught not taught. Sarah was about to marry Shaun, who adored her just like her daddy adored her mom. And now it's Shaun's turn to keep his admiring wife in beautiful cards and chocolate Kisses—forever.

Linda Newton

Full Confession

No one will get hurt—
just hand over the chocolate!
Karen Linamen

I hate to admit it, but I've sunk to an all-time low. Stealing—and from my own children. Wait, it gets worse. Stealing from my own children and then trying to cover my tracks. And worse still. Stealing from my own children, covering my tracks, and then repeating my hideous actions for nearly two weeks.

As a Sunday school teacher, I need to come clean.

At least I waited until after they had all gone to bed, and with eight children in our home, that is no easy feat. While the full moon cast iridescent shimmers of light, I quietly crept into their bedrooms, my breathing shallow, and scanned their little havens for their secret hiding spots. Because most mothers are also part detective, this wasn't too hard to accomplish.

Once I had homed in on the goods, I executed a swift heist, and slithered out their doorways, with the pale moonlight dancing on my back. As any thief will tell you, practice makes perfect, and if you don't get caught, who's going to know it happened in the first place?

The first couple of nights were the hardest, but once I was able to navigate their bedrooms in the pitch-black, each lift became a little bit easier, and by the end of the second week, I was operating like a professional cat burglar. I discarded the evidence each evening and defused my guilt by justifying that I was only borrowing from my kids, not stealing, and that I would repay them gradually, just as soon as I was able. My conscience bought into this rationalization for the entire duration of my loathsome behavior, which should have told me then and there that I had a serious problem and desperately needed to seek rehab.

My husband was the first to become suspicious of me because of all the extra time I was spending in our bathroom. I thought I was clever running the tub while I hid there, eating my stash, but raising eight kids had never afforded me the luxury of an hour-long soak prior to this, so after the seventh night, things just weren't adding up.

Soon after, my preteen children started asking if their younger siblings had been allowed in their bedrooms without permission. "Absolutely not," I reassured them. They bought into that for a couple of days but then started interrogating one another. Their bickering and raunchy accusations followed with fingers pointing in every direction except toward yours truly. I believe this is when my guilt first made its appearance. Watching my loving children tear one another's heads off for something that their sick mother had done started to take its toll on me. Not so much that I stopped cold turkey, however. No, I managed to put those hurtful images to the back of my head for several more nights as I shamefully continued to nourish my appalling habit.

By this time, I was afraid there was no hope for me. I was desperate to cry out for help, but too ashamed to admit what I'd done. I'd hit rock bottom. I could search the yellow pages for a support group, but what if it was too late? Could I be saved? Could I redeem myself to all eight of my children without any permanent damage?

Good news—yes, I could and I did! I gathered everyone together in our family room and made a full confession. Hard as it was, the tremendous sense of relief I felt once the burden was lifted felt much more exhilarating than the temporary highs I had been experiencing for the past two weeks since Halloween. That's what a chocolate obsession will do to an otherwise levelheaded, honest, and disciplined person.

Chocolate is indulgent, decadent, sometimes even intoxicating, and completely necessary to keep my senses alive and passionate. I know I can never live without it, but I also know I need to be a better role model for my children. I've promised them that next Halloween will be different. I won't steal from their hard-earned bags of candy, I will simply don a costume and go out and get my own. Trick or Treat!

Cheryl L. Butler

The Start of Something Great

The first recorded use of cacao dates back to 1000 BC to the Mesoamerican civilization. Chocolate didn't arrive in England until the early AD 1700s, and solid chocolate for eating wasn't developed until 1830.

It all begins with the cacao tree, an indigenous evergreen in Latin America. Its flowers grow right out of the trunk, often at the bottom of the tree. Some flowers bear football-shaped fruit, which is scored like a pumpkin and reddish-yellow in color. The seeds, or cacao beans, inside the fruit are the only thing used to make chocolate. The cacao beans are extracted, dried, and fermented in the sun and then shipped to manufacturers all over the world who take the dried, fermented seeds, now known as cocoa beans, and create chocolate.

Concocting the essence of unsweetened chocolate is quite simple. Chocolatiers roast, crush, then grind the cocoa beans between giant heated rollers to produce a ruddy-brown, satin-smooth liquor, very rich in cocoa butter, but very bitter to the taste. This chocolate essence is a pure food. Nothing is added to the beans, nothing is removed. The liquor is then poured into molds. Once it is cooled and wrapped, it is referred to as unsweetened chocolate, or baker's chocolate.

Cooks, bakers, and candy makers add sugar, vanilla, milk, nuts, fruits, and any number of other ingredients to the unsweetened chocolate to create treats that satiate our palettes and tantalize our taste buds.

Turtle Tales

Nine out of ten people like chocolate.
The tenth person always lies.

John Q. Tullius

I've been fascinated by turtles my whole life. Those little silver dollar–size turtles that crawled up and down my arms were my pets of choice when I was growing up. My dad even created Pat's Turtle Ranch in our backyard, fashioned out of an old tractor tire, complete with concrete rolling hills and craggy places for the turtles to climb and sun themselves.

Those live turtles were fun, but in my adult years I have to say that the best turtles of my life are not the ones in the Turtle Ranch or the giant ones I've snorkeled with in the ocean. No, my favorite turtles now are the ones my mother introduced me to as a child. The ones she kept out of reach on top of the refrigerator. *Turtles.* A rich chocolate, caramel, and pecan candy that's so good it's simply one of the most basic things that makes me happy.

Again, it was my dad, the Turtle Ranch builder, who got things off to a great start with the candy turtles. They were my mother's favorite sweet treat and usually on her birthday in November, Valentine's Day, Easter, and their anniversary in May, Dad would buy Mom a box of turtles, which she promptly placed on top of the refrigerator for safekeeping. If she was in a generous mood, every once in a while Mother would share one of her special turtle treats with me. Oh, was that ever a special day. I'd take one tiny bite and let that milk chocolate coating linger on my

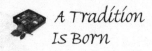

A Tradition Is Born

More than seventy years ago, an employee at the DeMet's Chocolate Factory (now owned by Nestlé) remarked to a fellow coworker that the company's new candy, an original recipe of real milk chocolate and creamy caramel with fresh pecans plainly visible from all sides, looked like a "turtle." The name stuck.

tongue. Then the caramel, sticky, rich, lip-smacking good. Finally the crunch of the pecans. Pure heaven.

For years I didn't have many turtle treats because my mother died when I was just thirty-four years old. But for some reason, without even knowing about my penchant for this luscious treat, my oldest son, Michael, bought me my very own box of turtles one year for my birthday in October.

Like my mother, I lovingly placed it on top of the refrigerator. Luckily, I had an empty nest by then and didn't feel obligated to share my treasure with anyone. I even learned to ration my turtles to one a day.

Thank goodness I raved about the turtles so much to Michael that he bought me another box for Christmas that year. He even had one waiting at his house for me next time I visited Wisconsin.

These days I'm still a turtle hoarder who looks forward to whatever holiday will remind Michael of my love of turtles.

I still enjoy the live cracker-eating turtles at the Turtle Deck not far from my home in Florida, but I have to say the melt-in-your-mouth, dreamy, creamy turtles that Michael surprises me with every so often are still my all-time favorites.

Life is good when you're surrounded by turtles.

Patricia Lorenz

"Alice, you really need to lay off the chocolate turtles!"

Reprinted by permission of Bruce Robinson. ©2007 Bruce Robinson.

A Guy Speaks Out for Chocolate

Chocolate-covered raisins, cherries, orange
slices, and strawberries all count as fruit, so
eat as many as you want.

Author Unknown

I t all started when I opened one of those tiny bite-size Dove Promise chocolates—you know, the ones wrapped in steamy romance novel red foil. The printed message inside the wrapper told me "It's definitely a bubble-bath day." At that moment it occurred to me: why does good chocolate have to be feminine? I mean, maybe I am a male chocoholic, but why does so much chocolate marketing exclude me? Why do I have to answer the question "How about a new dress?" or be told to "Give yourself a hug today. It just feels good." when I could be doing something that better suits my manly nature? That's why I've decided that it's time for a guy to speak out for chocolate.

Just to clarify, when I'm talking chocolate, I'm talking about the solid dark chocolate. Not the faint, diluted, disappointingly waxy flavor inside those foil-covered Easter bunnies, chocolate hearts, or chocolate lips. I'm talking the dark chocolate that makes you think you've just eaten a batch of hand-picked seeds of the cacao plant delivered from the jungles of Colombia to your front door on a burro. I'm talking about taste that lingers in my mouth, flooding my brain with a sea of cocoa flavonols.

But if you watch those TV ads, you'll see only legions of lingerie-draped or fashionably garbed women in Prada stilettos daintily tasting the chocolate, women closing their eyes in delight as they, and they alone, get to experience the secret pleasures of Dove or Godiva.

I'm proposing a similar liberation, and it's based on a simple premise: a guy should have chocolate rights, too. I hereby propose Dove Bites for Men, with messages for macho guys printed on the inside of a black foil wrapper. Why couldn't the Dove for Men wrappers say things like "It's definitely a weightlifting day," or "Thump your chest with your fist. It just feels good." There could be sayings for the sports-minded individual: "Let's you and me smack some hockey pucks," or "Wanna kickbox?" For the deeper thinkers, there could be a quasi-philosophical message like "One small chocolate for man, one giant chocolate for mankind." For the motor vehicle–inclined individual, wrappers could proclaim "There's a Ford 450 truck with a hemi in your near future," or "Have you hugged your modified Trans Am convertible today?" or "Isn't it about time you went to a demolition derby?"

If we equalized things this way, then a man wouldn't have to feel apologetic about walking into Wal-Mart, browsing a shelf loaded with stacks of bonbons and Hugs, then shrugging sheepishly at the checkout clerk when a half-dozen bags of dark chocolate glide down the conveyer belt. My campaign plan is a simple but fair one: chocolate for one, chocolate for all. In order to achieve balance in our society, we need to have equal bites. We need to be chocolately correct. Only then could a man boldly tear open a twelve-ounce cellophane package right there in the parking lot, toss a few pieces into his mouth, and proudly proclaim to the crowd of stunned shoppers looking on in surprise, "Free at last, free at last. Thank dark chocolate, I am free at last!"

Bill Meissner

Chocolate-Covered Cherries

Chocolate is nature's way of
making up for Mondays.

Anonymous

Working as a pinsetter at a bowling alley in 1949, I could make as much as forty-eight cents an hour—and in two hours I could make more than enough to buy a box of candy for my mother for her birthday. Centennial Bowling Alley, in my hometown of East Detroit, Michigan, paid twelve cents a game in cash at the end of the working day. In those days, automatic pinsetters were unknown. I was thirteen, and I needed sixty-nine cents for a box of chocolate-covered cherries on sale at Cunningham's Drugstore, a place where I often stopped on my way home from school.

Every day, my mother stood at the stove and fixed all the meals for everyone in our house—six kids, herself, and Grandpa. Grandpa had come to live with us after Grandma died. Wouldn't my mother like to eat something that, for once, she had not prepared herself? I thought so. And I had a plan how I could buy those chocolates.

On birthday Sunday, we all went to church in the morning. But instead of going home afterward, I walked directly to the bowling alley and signed in. Then I sat with a group of other young potential pinsetters. Unfortunately, on that Sunday in May, no bowlers showed up. By 4 PM the boss was doing crossword puzzles, so I signed out and headed for home.

Disappointed, I stopped at the drugstore to see if they had a job I could do to earn the box of chocolate-covered cherries. I had just opened the door when my younger brother rushed in. He said Mom had looked all over for me when I hadn't come home from church. Uh-oh! My mother was very intense in those days. I'd hear how she had searched all the hospitals and police stations.

Our black 1941 Hudson was parked at the curb. Ten pair of eyes belonging to my five siblings watched anxiously as I approached. I could feel them thinking, *Johnny's going to get it. Johnny's going to get it.* Well, it wouldn't be the first time. Mom had a hard grip on the steering wheel. "Where have you been?" she demanded, tight-lipped.

"At the bowling alley."

"You were throwing money away on bowling?" she asked sternly.

"I wanted to get a job setting pins."

"You aren't old enough for a work permit. You have to be fourteen."

"You don't need an ID to set pins."

"You should not be working on Sunday," she said, her voice harsh.

"I wanted to earn money to buy a present," I explained. "A box of chocolate-covered cherries with a red ribbon on it."

"A present? For someone at school?"

"For you, Mom. Today's your birthday."

Stunned is the only way to describe my mother's reaction. Her body stiffened. Then she became less tense, but she didn't cry. My mother never cried. Not when her mother got killed or when my father died fourteen months later. Not when social workers came and talked about taking us kids to various homes. Not even when she thought the bank was going to take her house. My mother was tough, but on this birthday, her hazel-colored eyes got really big . . . and wet. But she did not cry.

"I'm sorry I scared you, Mom," I said. "I just wanted to do something nice for your birthday." She sat looking at me, adult to child, mother to son, in the most intense, powerful moment we've ever shared. A bond grew. Slowly, she relaxed. Her birthday present was supposed to make her happy, and it did, eventually, but not in the way I had planned. We were all touched by her silence, the children in the backseat as well as the ones on the bench seat up front.

I got in and closed the door. Without talking, Mother turned the ignition key, pressed the starter button, and got the engine going. She worked the transmission lever and the clutch and we were soon rolling down Nine Mile Road toward home. We were almost to our turnoff before she said anything.

"When I was growing up," she said in a soft voice, "in farm country in Canada, birthdays were very important. My dad would make us toys—a sled or a wagon. Relatives would come over. No matter how poor we were or how busy she was, my sweet mother would bake a cake. This was around 1923. My mother would gather the eggs, sift the flour, and put sticks of wood in the stove. No thermostat in those days, either.

"She'd take time out to make me feel special with mittens she had knitted or a little doll or something. We had no birthday candles back then, so she put long matches in the cake. She did so much for me . . ." Mom took a deep breath.

"This is my first birthday without my mother. I thought about her all day, and when you didn't come home . . . how I miss her."

Now I was almost in tears. "Maybe I should bake a cake."

"Oh, no," Mom said. "What you did, going to work like that, to buy me something. That means you love me. I needed that reassurance. No one has done anything that nice for me in a long, long time. I would have liked that candy with the red ribbon."

"Happy birthday, Mom!" we all said. We were singing the birthday song as Mom pulled into the driveway.

Over the years, Mom had many more birthdays, and her children honored her with parties, gifts, and cakes that had real candles on them. Mom always sat in the guest-of-honor chair, and said, "I had angels! All of my children are angels!"

I corresponded with my mother many times during her later years as I gathered information for a family tree I was writing. She sent me names, dates, and pictures that helped. And Mom often wrote about the bowling alley job

I never got and the chocolate-covered cherries I never bought:

> ... *You wanted to set pins so that you could buy me that box of chocolate-covered cherries with a ribbon on top. That was the greatest birthday gift of all.*

Birthdays aren't just numbers beside names in my family. We've learned that it really is the thought that counts . . . and lasts.

John J. Lesjack

Oh, Fudge!

What you see before you, my friend,
is the result of a lifetime of chocolate.

Katharine Hepburn

One hot summer night in 1947, three very bored students—my sister, Betty, our roommate, Christy, and I sat around in our dorm room staring at one another. "I'm homesick," I confessed. "You know, for something fun to do."

After all, summer term wasn't the most exciting time of the year to be embroiled in books and reports and exams. Not when we could be swimming, partying, and picnicking. English Lit class was certainly no picnic or party. And this very ancient dorm in a sleepy Kentucky college town wasn't much of a picnic, either—especially up on the third floor under the rafters with no air conditioning.

"Yeah, me too," echoed Betty. "And starved, too. Let's make some fudge."

"Fudge?" cried Christy. "I adore fudge. But that would take a miracle."

Betty grinned and put a finger to her lips. "One miracle coming up. Promise not to tell," she said as she lifted up the bedspread that drooped down to the floor on all sides of her narrow dorm cot. Then from behind her shoes, suit-cases, and all the rest hidden under there, she started to pull out something as amazing as a magic wand: an old cooking pot, a measuring cup, a spoon—and an electric hotplate.

"Oh, boy!" Christy squealed.

"But we're not supposed to plug in hotplates," I cautioned.

"Well, just this once won't matter," Christy decided. "I mean, just think of it: fudge—real fudge. Gooey, melt-in-your-mouth, um-yummy chocolaty fudge. Doesn't it just make you drool?"

"But what are we going to make it out of?" I asked.

"Remember the story of 'Stone Soup'?" My sister grinned. "They wanted to make soup but didn't have anything to put in the pot but a stone. The townspeople started adding something until finally they had real soup. Well, why don't we see what the other girls on our floor can contribute?"

Right away we fanned out, looking for our missing magical ingredients. The food in our cafeteria was about as tasteless as it could get, and there was no snack shop open in the evening. So to keep from starving, most of our dorm mates stashed away food from the local supermarkets in their rooms.

One girl had a can of cocoa, another a bottle of syrup, another a stick of margarine. Several had sugar. One even had some milk that she kept to feed our dorm cat.

"That's it!" Betty cried. "Now we can make fudge!"

But she didn't carry back all those treasures alone—all

the donors came along, too. And so did everyone else on our floor. Soon a marvelous brew was stirring in the old pot. When we finally got it to the soft-ball stage, everyone giggled with delight.

The room was filled with the absolutely intoxicating glory of chocolate, floating out the open windows, and through the old-fashioned keyhole in the door. Then suddenly . . .

"Oh, no!" one girl cried. "I hear Miss Snorkel coming up the stairs! She must have smelled the chocolate."

The dorm had no elevator, and the old stairs from the first floor creaked with every step of her heavy feet. Our housemother was old and stern. She could put us all under detention.

Betty quickly shoved the electric hotplate, pot and all, back under her cot. "Everyone hide," Christy hissed.

But it was too late. "Betty, Bonnie, Christy, are you there?" our housemother barked.

Then she barged right in, facing a roomful of horror-stricken girls. Of course she couldn't see the hotplate, but the chocolate smell was overwhelming. The electric cord from the wall outlet just as conspicuously slipped right under my sister's bedspread.

She looked at us each in turn, scowling. Suddenly she laughed out loud. "I always liked fudge, too, girls," she announced. "Be sure to unplug the hotplate when you're through." Then she closed the door and left.

That was the most delicious fudge I ever ate in my life— what little I got, with so many gals to share it with. We even took a piece downstairs to Miss Snorkel. She didn't answer her door when we knocked, so we left it outside her door. The next morning her piece was gone. She even went around all day with a bit of chocolate on her ample chin. Right underneath her smile.

Bonnie Compton Hanson

Sweet Chocolate Sunshine

Strength is the capacity to break a
chocolate bar into four pieces with your
bare hands—and then eat
just one of the pieces.

Judith Viorst

Here in India, for a rich child, buying a bar of chocolate is a carefree act, but for the poor kid, it's
manna. Chocolate is a rare treat. In all likelihood, he can't
even afford to spend the meager five rupees for this object
of utmost desire. Chocolate, in this country, is a preroga-
tive of the rich. The poor don't have chocolate. It's just not
done.

The streets of Calcutta are filled with begging children.
I don't give them money because I know that most of this
money doesn't go to them anyway, and yet the sadness in
their eyes tugs at my heartstrings. Instead, when I see a
little child begging, I buy him a bar of chocolate. There is
one child outside my college who has befriended me and
says "Hi!" to me every time I walk past. His name, as I
found out much later, is Raja.

On an impulse one day, I bought him a bar of Dairy
Milk. As he took it from my hand his eyes lit up. The

moment he held that bar of chocolate in his hands it was as though he had struck gold. Gratitude overwhelmed him, and he became shy and ran off, but not before muttering a very excited, "Thank you, Didi!" (In Hindi *didi* is used to refer to an elder sister.)

A little surprised by his immense joy, I watched him for a bit while he proudly showed off his newest acquisition to his friends, some of whom were wide-eyed, while the naughtier ones tried to grab at it but obviously failed. After his initial euphoria wore off and the other children started to get bored and walked away, he called them back. He slowly unwrapped the thin foil covering to reveal dark brown chocolate, while the rest watched, drooling, in mystified silence.

What a show-off, I thought. But right then, he did something I couldn't have imagined. He broke the bar into five equal pieces and shared them with all his friends, who now treated him like nothing less than a demigod. I would have thought that this little kid would want to keep the chocolate, this rare treat, all to himself.

I bought him a chocolate bar many times after that, and I really did think he would get greedy after a while, but he always divided it equally amongst all his friends. I even tried buying him a really small bar on one particular occasion, but somehow they all managed to get a bite out of that as well.

Before buying the chocolate for him on one of those many days, I asked him why he always shares his chocolate. He answered in such a matter-of-fact manner that made me feel a little ashamed. He simply said, "Didi, they're my family; we're supposed to share everything, big or small. I couldn't dream of something without sharing it with all of them. Why do you ask? Wouldn't you do the same with your family or friends?" With this, he took the chocolate from my hand, shouted a delighted "Thank you!" (his shyness has disappeared over the weeks), and skipped down the sidewalk to find his family.

Had I become selfish? Had I become too caught up with myself to even care about sharing my joys, my possessions, my achievements, my sorrows, my failures . . . my life? Did I care about those I loved most? Did they even think of me when they had something to share, or did they just keep it to themselves? Raja's words kept ringing in my ears.

Sometimes our smallest acts bring sunshine into someone's life, and that sunshine automatically overflows into our own lives, too.

Radhika Basu Thakur

Bittersweet Birthday

Other things are just food.
But chocolate's chocolate.

Patrick Skene Catling

O n my daughter Emma's first birthday, the temperature was five below zero, typical for January in Minnesota. I was determined to bake her a chocolate layer cake. (Was the cake really for the one-year-old, or was it for the chocolate-addicted mommy, you may ask?)

"Mom, we can't bake a cake for Emma," my older kids yelled, rushing to the refrigerator to help stir up the birthday surprise. "We're out of eggs."

"We'll just drive up to the corner store, buy eggs, and bake that birthday cake in no time," I explained, stuffing all three kids into their coats, hats, mittens, and boots.

For the love of chocolate, how could the kids think a little thing like a lack of eggs would hinder Emma's birthday celebration? I shoveled the six inches of accumulating snow from the sidewalk, scooped up Emma from a snow bank, and led the parade to our aging Pontiac. Emma would get her chocolate birthday cake, snow or no snow.

Our car, however, had other plans. Moaning and

sputtering like a sick cat, the car's engine refused to turn over. We were stuck in a snowstorm without a birthday cake. Eyes tearing with disappointment, I looked through the flurried sky toward our local convenience store just a few blocks away.

Under the same circumstances today, a few children later, I'd merely shrug and concede, "We'll make birthday instant chocolate pudding." Maybe I'd call a neighbor and bum a few eggs. But I was young then, passionate and strong-willed. Plus, I really had a craving for chocolate cake.

Suddenly, some motherly instinct akin to insanity flared inside me. Obtaining those eggs became a personal conquest, like climbing an obscenely high mountain. Nothing—not five-below weather or a dead car battery— would prevent me from baking that chocolate birthday cake for myself . . . er, Emma.

"Let's sled!" offered my five-year-old.

"Yep," I agreed, "sledding is just the thing." Plopping the older girls in our pink plastic toboggan, I trudged to the store through knee-deep snowdrifts like a mindless work-horse yoked to a pathetic pink plastic plow.

Emma, the birthday girl, was strapped to me in a front-pack, bundled in a teeny-weeny snowsuit and flannel blanket. She began to cry even before we made it to our own mailbox. "It's all right, Emma Bemma," I consoled. Peeking under her blanket, I kissed her firm little cheeks. She stopped crying when I kissed her, so I kissed her a lot.

We made it to Conoco and bought a dozen grade A large eggs. My numb fingers tossed spare change on the counter, and then we started for home. Zipped inside my jacket, nestled between my warm breasts like a new puppy, Emma snoozed. The other two girls giggled, savoring falling snowflakes, dragging their mittened hands along the side of the sled, smearing the snow like white frosting on a cake.

I, in turn, pulled the load, panting like a fat lady dancing at her cousin's wedding reception. At home, baby Emma napped while the other children helped me whip up the most fantastic chocolate layer cake ever conceived. Emma would get her birthday cake.

Later that evening, as our little family chirped "Happy Birthday to You" in the glow of a single candle, I noticed how rosy Emma's cheeks appeared. Perfect circles of crimson smacked Emma's skin where I had kissed her in the cold. My wet, well-intentioned kisses must have frozen my baby's face. In addition to the Midwest's best chocolate layer cake, I had given my baby frostbite for her first birthday.

This March, we will celebrate my son's first birthday. We'll host lunch for a pack of sugar-high toddlers, rip open some colorfully wrapped packages: dump trucks, action figures, books. Then the grand finale—the birthday cake. I'll parade around with an exquisite chocolate layer cake topped with a single flickering birthday candle. My little boy will glow in the love, the affection, the attention. He'll love his cake.

And don't worry, this time I've thought of everything. On his first birthday, no matter what tricks Mother Nature plays, my son will still dive into a succulent, rich, super-moist chocolate layer cake. Choice of mocha, semisweet, bittersweet, or dark chocolate frosting. Nine-inch cake serves twelve. Special this month.

Thankfully, on this baby's birthday, the grocery store delivers.

Cristy Trandahl

Life Is Short—Eat Chocolate

Chocolate lovers are going to eat chocolate whether it's good for us or not. But when a study on chocolate comes up with a whole new theory about how good chocolate is for us, well, it's like the Fourth of July. Send up the rockets! More pleasure, less guilt. Here are just a few of those marvelous discoveries:

- Chocolate contains high levels of phenol, which helps fight heart disease.

- When we eat chocolate, our brains produce serotonin, the "feel good" chemical.

- Three chemicals found specifically in dark chocolate—epicatechin, gallic acid, and flavonoids—are thought to protect our hearts and reduce blood pressure. However, because it's high in sugar and fat, in order to eat a bit of chocolate every day, reduce calories in other areas.

- Chocolate does not cause acne. Pure chocolate contains anti-oxidants, which actually aid in producing better skin complexion. Some experts believe the milk mixed with the chocolate is actually the culprit.

- Research shows evidence that flavonol-rich cocoa stimulates neurovascular activity, enhancing memory and alertness.

- An entire ounce of chocolate contains no more caffeine than a cup of decaffeinated coffee.

- Chocolate triggers the release of endorphins, which reduce the body's sensitivity to pain.

- Medical complaints that have been treated with chocolate include anemia, poor appetite, mental fatigue, tuberculosis, fever, gout, kidney stones, reduced longevity, and poor sexual appetite.

- A study at Cornell University found hot cocoa has nearly twice the antioxidants of red wine and three times the amount found in green tea.

A Nickel and Chocolate Cake with Candy-Bar Icing

What use are cartridges in battle?
I always carry chocolate instead.

George Bernard Shaw

I lived with my parents on the same farm with my grandparents but in a separate house. My grandmother's mother died when I was two years old. Grandma never talked about her family, so I assumed that she had none.

One Sunday evening, after the milking was done, we were running the milk through the big cream separator when she said, "I had the best cake today. It was dark chocolate with candy-bar icing."

"What's candy-bar icing?" I queried as my mouth began to water and my brain began to imagine this masterpiece. I began scheming as to how I might get some of it.

"Gertie came to see me today. She always baked the best cakes and she makes a topping out of chocolate candy bars that is just heavenly," Grandma replied as she poured another pail of milk into the strainer on top of the separator bowl. As she leaned back against the wall, I thought that I detected a tear playing around the corner of her eye.

"Who's Gertie?" I asked.

She told me that Gertie was her only surviving sister and that they had not spoken since their mother's funeral fifteen years earlier, even though they had been very close while growing up. I was surprised but knew my grandmother could be very stubborn sometimes.

She said that her sister had apologized for being resentful of my grandmother for getting all of their mother's insurance money when she died. Gertie said that over the years she had come to realize that my grandmother had taken care of their mother, fed her, and nursed her in her final illness. She told her that she now realized that their mother was destitute when my grandparents had taken her in, and that Grandma was entitled to the insurance money.

Grandma had not said a word, but walked into her bedroom and returned with a cigar box and handed it to her sister. Gertie opened the box containing two objects, a receipt for their mother's funeral in the amount of $399.95 and a nickel.

"What's this?" Gertie asked.

"Mother had a $400 insurance policy, with the funeral director as the beneficiary. The funeral bill was $399.95. This is the exact nickel that the funeral director gave me in change, and I have kept it for you all these years so that you would have something from our mother!" my grandma replied.

Gertie could not believe that she had allowed fifteen

years of birthday parties, holidays, sisterly sharing, and caring go by over a nickel.

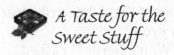

A Taste for the Sweet Stuff

From that day on Grandma and her sister made up for lost time with many more chocolate cakes with candy-bar icing. Grandma seemed a lot happier after that day, and I gained a great-aunt that I did not even know existed, as well as a steady supply of chocolate cakes with candy-bar icing.

The best chocolate contains at least 55 percent cocoa solids, which contribute to the bittersweet flavor. But more than 90 percent of Americans prefer milk chocolate, which is sweeter, higher in fat, and lower in cocoa solids than bittersweet or dark chocolate.

We all learned that pride is more easily swallowed with anything chocolate.

Bill Satterlee

Sweet Shoppe

Look, there's no metaphysics on earth like chocolates.

Fernando Pessoa

"Where are we going, Mommy?" Adrienne would ask. The answer was usually the same. "We're going shopping, honey."

My three kids and I spent most Saturday nights in the mall when they were young. Our finances were tight, and sometimes extra money was at a premium, but shopping was our escape. We could deal with our life during the week when we were busy, but come Saturday night we were face-to-face with reality.

Psychologists say there's an elevation of mood, a touch of serenity for some when they are buying or acquiring things. I wanted my children and me to have that feeling after my husband, their father, had recently died. It had been a long, lingering death that took its toll on the entire family. We needed to feel better, so we used shopping trips together as an outlet for our grief. That may sound strange to some, and even though we did more window-shopping than buying, it worked for us. With the bright lights and other people at the mall intent on their own needs and desires, we could fit right in. No one knew that we were grieving. We were just shoppers, like everyone else.

Our treat on each outing was a visit to a candy shop. Most often it was one where the kids could choose their favorite candy—gummy bears, Swedish fish, or Good & Plenty. However, when I knew that their loss was affecting them more deeply, we'd go to the candy counter at the upscale department store, where each of the kids would choose one lovely piece of gourmet chocolate. We lingered over the glass-fronted counter, looking at each beautifully made confection. The kids would make a different selection each time, but mine was always a dark, dark chocolate shell filled with more dark, creamy chocolate. The aroma, texture, and taste of the chocolate transported us. It always put us in a better mood, and as I discovered recently, I was making good memories for my children.

A bit of sugared candy or bite of chocolate wasn't much, but it satisfied a need. Our need to buy something? No. Our need to be together—our need for something sweet in our lives.

Patricia Carroll Johnson

A Good Chocolate Is Hard to Find

A true chocolate lover finds ways
to accommodate his passion
and make it work with his lifestyle.

Julie Davis

I n the summer of 1992, I made my first and only trip to Salzburg, Austria—a fortunate side trip I was able to squeeze in while shooting videos for the Corps of Engineers at U.S. Army bases in southern Germany.

As I roamed the narrow streets of this romantic medieval city, I was struck by the unusual marriage of classical music history and modern tourism. Almost every storefront window in the city's center was brimming with chocolates tightly wrapped in bright red and gold foil bearing the likeness of Salzburg's favorite son: Wolfgang Amadeus Mozart. The irony was not lost on me that a man who was impoverished at the time of his death and buried in an unmarked grave in Vienna was making so much money for local chocolatiers.

My skepticism transformed into marvel once I entered a candy shop and actually tasted a Mozart kugel. The rich layers of flavors might be an acquired taste for American consumers. Each ball-shaped kugel was filled with pistachio marzipan and hazelnut nougat, dipped in both milk and dark chocolate. And since European chocolate has a higher butterfat content than its American counterpart, the smooth richness of the double chocolate coating was incomparable. I had never tasted anything like it; after just one kugel, I was hooked faster than I could say *Eine Kleine Nachtmusik*. If there ever was a chocolate worthy of a world-renowned composer such as Mozart, this was it.

Before I left Salzburg, I bought enough Reber Mozart Kugel to nibble on the plane ride back to the United States and share with my immediate family in suburban Chicago. I still had one kugel left when I returned to my sparsely furnished, one-bedroom apartment in downstate Champaign, Illinois. I initially intended to save the precious piece of candy for a special occasion, but at that particular point in my life I had few reasons for actual celebration. As I updated my résumé in my apartment during one of my many solitary Saturday nights, I consumed the remaining piece of kugel, savoring every last bite of the silky hazelnut crème and chewy marzipan. Afterward, I neatly folded the glittering wrapper as a souvenir. I assumed that I'd never taste another Mozart chocolate until I had the chance to return to Europe.

Four years later I was back in Chicago, in the hopes of advancing my career as well as my social life. On a brisk Saturday night in mid-March, I met a young man named Greg at a party, and our conversation lasted until our hosts started to motion everyone toward the door. By the end of the evening, Greg invited me to join him for a concert the following weekend at the Chicago Symphony Orchestra. I was very impressed—and a little intimidated—at the prospect of having a first date at the symphony. My knowledge of classical music was rather limited at that time. After the concert performance, I knew that I would be unable to discuss the finer points of Mozart's music, but I couldn't help but mention the wonderful Mozart chocolate I had enjoyed years earlier. As it turned out, Greg had also sampled Mozart kugel while he was passing through Vienna during a bike tour of Europe.

On our next date, Greg presented me with something he had found in a German deli in his neighborhood on the north side of Chicago: a Reber Mozart Piano Bar, which was a candy bar-size version of the original Mozart kugel, with the added crunchy sensation of crisped rice cereal blended into the chocolate coating. The combination of flavors was just as delicious as I remembered it. Not only had I discovered a place where I could find Mozart chocolate close to home, but also I had found someone with whom I could share it.

Three years later, Greg and I ordered 250 medallion-size Mozart chocolates from another local German deli so we could distribute them as favors for our wedding guests.

Robyn Kurth

Love at First Truffle

It's not that chocolates are a substitute for
love. Love is a substitute for chocolate.
Chocolate is, let's face it,
far more reliable than a man.

Miranda Ingram

"Y ou'll never meet Mr. Right," my friends warned,
"as long as you're attached to Mr. Wrong." While I
knew that was probably true, there nevertheless
hovered the angst I'd never meet anyone besides Dick.

Disheartened by the prospect of another Christmas
without a commitment, I opted for a radical change of
scenery. Scotland, to be specific. The coworker who joined
me—and who shared the popular view that Dick was a
twit—saw it as a chance to research her ancestry. I saw it
as a chance to not only contemplate a murky future, but
also give Dick plenty of time to miss me.

The first few days were earmarked for sightseeing
around London, an excursion that included a side-trip to
Bath, a magical place that dates back to the Romans and
was popularized by native hot springs rumored to yield
strange, mystical powers. Quicker than you could say, *"Et
tu?"* off came the togas, in came the tourists, and Bath

today still looks pretty much like the spa of yore to which Romans retreated after each season of pillaging.

Just before lunch our guide directed us to the final sight on the tour—a large, indoor barrel that looked like a rustic hot tub. "The legend about this pool," she explained, "is that whatever you wish for will come true." My companion cautioned me to wish wisely. Obviously she knew I was going to wish for Dick to come to his senses.

"The problem with putting an actual name on a wish," she said, "is that it cuts out other potential candidates who could meet the same criteria."

Fortunately, I was in a listening mood. I closed my eyes and made the request, "May there be a knight in shining armor when I return, and may our love be true and everlasting."

To my dismay, only two messages were on my machine from Dick when I came home. The first was to say how much he missed me and that he was definitely going to be thinking of talking about maybe making a commitment. The second was that he had run into his ex-wife, Estelle, he was joining her on vacation at Lake Tahoe, and he would call me when he got back.

I dragged myself into the office on Monday, still suffering the effects of yet another punch in the heart. It was pouring rain. I remember that because the first stranger who came through the door was wearing a much-sprinkled Western-style overcoat and hat. What I noticed first, though, was that he had the kindest smile and sparkling blue eyes. Apparently my eyes caught his attention, too, and he complimented me on them.

"In the moment you said thank you," Mark later told

me, "I felt as if I knew everything there was to know about you."

Because he was going to visit our office frequently, he asked if he would have to call each time for an appointment. I told him I could be bribed with chocolate.

A See's Candy was conveniently located two doors down the street. The handsome stranger became a regular customer. No matter what kind of day I was having, my spirits always lifted whenever Mark walked in. I'd find myself saving up my funniest stories to share with him, just to prolong his being there.

I assumed a man as nice as this one was probably married. He assumed I was spoken for as well. It wouldn't have been appropriate, he later explained, to have a personal relationship with someone in an office where he had business as a lobbyist.

On Valentine's Day 1997, it was cold and raining, and I had as little prospect for romance as I did three years previous. Dick, it turned out, had not only gravitated back to Estelle, but also kept insisting it was only temporary.

Near closing time, the door opened and in walked Mark. "These are for you," he announced, handing me a red box from See's containing six of my favorite truffles. What I didn't know was that he was handing me more than a box of chocolates; he was handing me his heart. I also didn't know that he, too, was going home to an empty house that evening.

I had just been given a promotion to a field office closer to home. On the one hand, I was glad to escape the cost of downtown parking. On the other hand, I was going to miss that weekly truffle fix. I gave him my new number when we parted.

"Maybe we can stay in touch," I said.

No one was more surprised than I when he called in April and asked if he could take me to lunch for my birthday at an elegant restaurant in the city's historic district. I turned to face the courtyard gate at the precise moment he walked in. And in that sunlit, movie-magic moment, he couldn't wait any longer to declare his feelings. That afternoon he asked me to become his wife and I accepted. The irony was that we hadn't even exchanged our first kiss, much less gone on a first date. We just knew.

One year later, we exchanged our vows at Stirling Castle, honeymooned in the Scottish Highlands, and began the happily-ever-after I always dreamed of . . . and wished for. And, yes, he still brings me chocolate.

Christina Hamlett

Chocolate Attack

I never met a chocolate I didn't like.

Marina Sirtis as Deanna Troi,
Star Trek: The Next Generation

M any years ago I went to San Francisco with my husband where we were invited for cocktails by a couple who resided in an apartment with three walls of windows overlooking the city and the Bay. The apartment was beautiful, the hosts affable and kind, but the only thing that has stuck in my mind all these years was the comment by the woman that she allowed herself one Hershey's Kiss each day.

I have rather regular chocolate urges myself and have never found that one Hershey's Kiss, no matter how delicious, would satisfy the need. Weeks later, I was in the supermarket and the craving for chocolate became intense. I tried to distract myself by handpicking a bag of cherries and a tub of blueberries, both of which I like very much. I also picked up a cauliflower, a few peppers, bananas, and a purple onion. I was certain that these good-for-you foods would diminish my craving.

The candy was in the aisle with pasta, so if I needed pasta I must traverse this aisle. I felt confident enough to enter at the candy end of the aisle, feeling my chocolate urge had abated. As luck would have it, the large bag of Hershey's Kisses was on sale, noted in bold black letters. I stopped and picked up a bag. It molded itself around my hand as if asking to go home with me. I put it down and it called to me, "You can eat just one."

At that moment I glanced at all the fruits and vegetables, and then nonchalantly placed one bag of Kisses in with them. I went about my shopping, getting what we needed. There was meat and cheese and milk and rolls and paper goods. I could take or leave any of them, but as each item was added to the cart, I thought about putting the Hershey's Kisses back on the shelf.

I thought of the woman in San Francisco and told myself, *If she could do it, so can I,* and put the candy on the counter with the rest of my groceries. I got home and unloaded the things from the car and proceeded to put them away. Some went to the refrigerator, some to the pantry, and then the chocolate Kisses were in my hands. Where could I put them? *Well, silly,* I told myself, *put them in the pantry with everything else. You're going to have only one, for goodness sake.* So away they went.

It was a little after noon and I was getting hungry. I pride myself on having a light lunch. I even brag about it. When my husband gets home, he brags about his light lunch. We exchange brags. On this day I had low-fat cottage cheese with fresh honeydew melon and cherry-flavored seltzer water. I finished it, felt strong, and decided to open the Kisses and have just one.

I got the package out of the cupboard, took scissors and

cut off one corner. Two silver Kisses slid out of the bag. I laid the bag down and picked up the candy. *Well, two won't hurt,* I thought. After all, I had a light lunch. I opened the silver foil, watched it fall to the table along with the little piece of paper with "Kisses" printed down it. I put the chocolate into my mouth and felt it warm and melt as I slid it to one side to chew it. The second went down just as easily. The bag was still on the table so I decided to have just a couple more while I read the paper. The hole in the bag had gotten a little bigger and four Kisses tumbled out. Well, I would just nibble these while I read.

By the time I finished reading the paper, a pile of silver foil was beside me and all those little strips of paper. I was horrified and ashamed. I scooped them all up and crushed them into a little ball, then buried them in the garbage. I got a twist tie from the drawer and closed the bag of Kisses. Before putting it back in the cupboard, I reluctantly read the calorie panel on the side of the bag. In eight pieces, there are 210 calories. I liked the straightforward look of that. There was no figuring out a serving size or anything. If you ate eight Hershey's Kisses you consumed 210 calories.

I wasn't sure how many I had eaten, and I had made the wrappers disappear so I couldn't check, and besides, I didn't want to know. The damage was done. I gave myself a good talking to. I decided that the woman in San Francisco had to be exaggerating, although she didn't seem the type. I told myself I didn't transgress every day, and, after all, I wouldn't want Hershey's to go out of business.

My husband came home and told me he had tuna salad with lettuce, tomato, and onion. I told him I had cottage cheese and fruit.

There have to be certain secrets in a marriage. Don't tell me I'm wrong. We have been married just over thirty years. Chocolate upsets my husband. He thinks it's evil and glowers when I suggest getting fudge. "How could you?" he might say, and I don't. It's better if I indulge alone. Why upset the man?

I know it is not possible to eat one Hershey's Kiss, and I have three quarters of a bag still left in my pantry. I can better eat none than one, so I decided to put the rest of the bag in the freezer, and when another chocolate attack grips me, I'll extract that bag from the freezer—and enjoy!

Lynne MacKnight

A Taste of Chocolate

Giving chocolate to others is an intimate
form of communication, a sharing
of deep, dark secrets.

Milton Zelman

I t was Valentine's Day 1963, and I was a twenty-
four-year-old soldier stationed at Fort Bragg,
North Carolina, getting ready to undergo four
weeks of Airborne training and six weeks of Special Forces
training. At one in the afternoon I was called into the
orderly room and handed a telegram.

*Surprise! Will be arriving at 3:00 PM, February 14,
Piedmont Airport, Fayetteville. Can hardly wait.
Love, Lynne.*

I had no idea she would be coming early. As a matter of
fact, we'd planned to wait until my training was completed
before she would arrive. Now I had less than two hours to
rent a place to live in and buy essentials. Luckily, the com-
manding officer understood and gave me the use of the
company jeep.

By that afternoon I managed to rent a forty-foot trailer
for thirty dollars per month, purchase a used set of dishes,
cookware, and flatware from a local pawn shop, and buy an

inexpensive set of linens. The run-down trailer park catered to lower-ranking enlisted men. After giving the landlord first and last months' rent, I had twenty-five dollars left and payday was two weeks away. I'd forgotten about food. Maybe we could live on love.

Oh, that trailer! I wouldn't dare have the audacity to call it a mobile home. It was simply a large travel trailer painted a garish red and white. The interior was done in cheap blond paneling, and the flowered linoleum floor was pitted and scraped, showing the weathered plywood subfloor.

The furnishings consisted of a small battered couch against the end wall and a scarred coffee table with one loose leg. To the left of the living room was the kitchen. A stained sink, a tiny electric stove that needed cleaning, and a battered Formica-topped table completed the ensemble. Further down the hallway was the bathroom, whose door had been replaced by a shower curtain. At the far end of the trailer was the bedroom—just enough room for a built-in closet, a chest of drawers, and a double bed with a sagging mattress.

This was to be our home, and I was ashamed to even show it to Lynne. I held my breath as I opened the flimsy trailer door, watching her face for any change of expression. "I didn't have time to buy any food and we don't have much money, Lynne," I said apologetically. "Payday isn't for another two weeks, and I know this isn't what you expected, and I'm sorry. . ." I ran on until she put her finger to my lips.

"Shh. I know, darling. I have some money with me. We'll manage until then."

"But you don't know the worst part," I replied. "I have to go back to the barracks. They have bed check at night and I have to live there until we get married. That means you'll be here all alone."

She looked up smiling radiantly at me. "Then I guess we'd better get married as soon as we can."

"What's this?" she queried, spying the Hershey's bar wrapped with a narrow red ribbon I had placed on the table.

K-Ration Delicacy

Since the days of the American War for Independence, chocolate has been part of a soldier's rations. Chocolate, at least the essence of chocolate made from crushed cacao tree beans, is a highly concentrated food source, small in bulk and easy to carry.

Today, chocolate is considered more of a sweet dessert treat than a serious food source.

"Oh, nothing. Just a little housewarming present," I replied sheepishly. "Just wish it could be more."

"It's perfect," she said, picking up the candy as she sat on the couch. She reached for my hand, and I sat next to her as she unwrapped it. We shared it in silence and kisses, not needing to talk, and I looked into those beautiful blue eyes of hers and could see her love for me reflected in them. A week later we were married. That evening I fixed pancakes and eggs for dinner, and for dessert we had a Hershey's bar.

Every anniversary for the last forty-four years a chocolate candy bar has been the cornerstone of our celebration. It symbolizes the struggles we endured as a young married couple with little to share. No matter what we give each other for anniversary presents, a Hershey's bar with that original red ribbon from those many years ago remains our favorite. I'm amazed how her beautiful blue eyes still sparkle with love as she unwraps it and we share it together in loving silence.

Gary Luerding

"My ideal man is kind, sensitive, intelligent, six-two, a hundred-eighty pounds, and made of solid milk chocolate."

Reprinted by permission of Patrick Hardin. ©1998 Patrick Hardin.

Some Like It Hot

The taste of chocolate is a sensual pleasure
in itself, existing in the same world as sex.

Dr. Ruth Westheimer

I t was December. Christmas was just around the cold front. I huddled at the kitchen table, scanning sales circulars and sipping hot chocolate while I waited for the babysitter. I had a list and an envelope that didn't have to strain much to hold the results of cashing my paycheck. In the months since my divorce, I finally had the chance to show I could manage finances without muddling up the black ink and red ink columns in the checkbook. A liberating, terrifying prospect. But there's just something about cradling a mug of steaming hot chocolate topped with marshmallows to make you believe in flying reindeer. I drained the cup and watched the last few drops of chocolate settle in the bottom. The babysitter's car splashed through the slushy puddle in the driveway. Time to "Jingle Bell Rock."

A telephone call halted the process. Bill was a family friend, the best man at my wedding years before. I knew him in the days when irreconcilable differences was something you read about in Dear Abby. A confirmed bachelor

Presidential Sweet Tooth

Before he became president, Abraham Lincoln had a grocery store in Illinois. When researchers studied his faded bookkeeping records, they discovered that the only packaged and advertised food product sold in his store was Baker's Breakfast Cocoa.

Thomas Jefferson was also a great fan of hot chocolate.

since his own divorce, he was an old hand at meeting the holiday season as a lone elf. In the meantime, he fed my sons' ravenous Dr. Seuss appetites and checked periodically to make sure the kitchen cupboard wasn't bare. His idea to brave the Christmas crowds together was a welcome one, and his offer to serve as chauffeur even more so. I hate to drive in December. Once Santa cruises into town, there's no place to park at the mall. You wouldn't think a miniature sleigh and eight tiny reindeer would take up so much space.

For me, shopping is an all-or-nothing deal. If it's not a good day, I couldn't find a bargain with a mall map and a three-day supply of food-court coupons. But today everything ran smoother than a melted chocolate bar. We compared prices, we stood in line, and we tucked treasures into shopping bags so full they looked like pouches of microwave popcorn just before the timer rings. Somewhere in between the candy canes and Christmas socks, in the middle of the crowds and the cash registers, we began to hold hands.

By the end of the day, my list was done. For someone who takes a week to choose the red sweater over the green and still has to settle the question with an impromptu poll among random passersby, this was indeed a Christmas miracle.

Contented, I collapsed on a bench outside a mall coffee shop. With a wink, Bill plunged into the crowd once more, and as I waited, I tried to guess the prizes in the boxes and bags that scurrying shoppers carried. Christmas waits last longer than other kinds, but I hardly noticed as I perched on our bench surrounded by treasures. He reappeared before long, bearing a cup of steaming hot chocolate for me and coffee for him. As the smell of holiday magic wafted out of our cups, we laughed and talked and watched the crowd together. Flying reindeer? Who wouldn't believe?

Bill and I were married the next summer. Ten years later, we still brave the crowds together at Christmas. He still sips his coffee while I warm up inside and out with hot chocolate. We watch the passing shoppers and make a game of guessing what's in their packages. And I still believe.

Amy Mullis

Chocolate Milk and Bologna

*The divine drink, which builds up resistance
and fights fatigue. A cup of this precious
drink (cocoa) permits a man to walk for a
whole day without food.*

Montezuma II, Aztec Emperor

I'm sure my mother never considered chocolate milk and bologna sandwiches part of the family legacy. Instead, it was probably just a survival technique for a mother of thirteen kids who had to find a quick meal while out on the road.

Once a month, we would make the one-hour drive from our small Texas town into San Antonio for major shopping. The minimum three stops we always made were Fed Mart, New York Fabrics, and the bread store for twenty loaves of day-old bread. My mother usually toted about four or five kids with her on these trips. I'm not sure if it was because she didn't trust leaving all of us at home, or because she needed us to push the shopping carts at Fed Mart because we always filled more than one.

Sometime during the day, we'd need to eat. We'd go to a grocery store and buy a loaf of bread, a package of bologna, and chocolate milk. At home, we always made chocolate milk with cocoa, sugar, and milk—which guaranteed inconsistency and little crunchy pieces of sugar toward the end. Store-bought chocolate milk was like drinking velvet. It was thick, rich, and consistent every time.

Fast-forward thirty years and I have my own family of five kids. In the early days of our trips out and about, I would prepare a well-balanced lunch and pack it in the ice chest. We'd have a protein, a vegetable, a starch, and juice drinks. One day I did not have time to pack a meal and actually left the house empty-handed (gasp!). About lunchtime, getting desperate to feed my family, I remembered my humble beginnings and those meals right out of the grocery bag. I found out that day that a loaf of bread and a package of bologna still works in a pinch. And store-bought chocolate milk is still like drinking velvet.

Stephanie Buckwalter

2

TICKLING THE TASTE BUDS

The Treasure Hunt

Chocolate: The damnable agent of
necromancers and sorcerers.

Fifteenth-century French cleric

I n September, 1992, I quit a job that had been paying me a respectable salary to live on my savings while I got serious about starting a work-at-home business.

It was wonderful! Armed with bags of real chocolate malted milk balls, chocolate-covered raisins, and frozen Snickers, I began my new career. I enjoyed leisurely cups of tea in the morning while I watched the *Today* show. I soon realized that I didn't even have to get dressed. I could slop around in my sweatshirt and baggy red pajama bottoms all day if I wanted to.

"What's this?" I said aloud to myself as I flipped TV channels. "A talk show? I love talk shows!"

After the talk shows I'd water the plants, paint another sweatshirt for my Christmas gift collection, talk to my unemployed nurse friend on the phone for an hour, put a load of clothes in the washer, feed the birds, make spaghetti sauce, run errands, eat another handful of malted milk balls.

"Whoa, lunch time already?" Time for another TV talk show. More phone calls. Well, you get the picture. Very often I didn't get to my home office until 3 PM, and more often than not I didn't get there at all.

But I was having a ball. That winter I welcomed hosts of out-of-town friends and relatives. I stocked up on my chocolate collection, *for my guests*, I rationalized.

After weeks of not setting foot inside my office or even turning on my computer, I started to feel like a slug. The extra ten pounds on my frame didn't help my mood either.

One day at the drugstore I picked up six chocolate candy bars, three for me and three for my thirteen-year-old son, Andrew, my only child still at home.

When I got home I sat down at the kitchen counter and decided it would be fun to send Andrew on a treasure hunt for his candy. I cut a sheet of paper into eight pieces. On the first I wrote, "There's a tasty prize for you at the end of the Mama Lorenz treasure hunt. The first clue is at the place that rhymes with *bears*."

Taped to one of the upper stairs was the next clue. "Clue number three is not on this floor. But it is near the door. Look up!"

Andrew ran upstairs and down looking for and finding his clues, laughing all the way. He was having as much fun on his treasure hunt as I had writing and hiding the clues.

Clue number eight said, "You're tired, right? Go to bed. Hug your pillow. Dream sweet dreams and enjoy your prize. I love you. Mom." He found the chocolate bars inside his pillow.

After a big hug and giant "Thanks, Mom!" Andrew stood next to the kitchen counter where I was watching *Oprah* on the kitchen TV.

My son put his arm around my shoulders, held out the eight slips of paper with the treasure hunt clues, and paused for a moment before he said, "So, Mom, is this what you do now instead of earning money?"

His simple question hit me hard. The eight clues I'd written for Andrew's little treasure hunt were the first words I'd actually written in months. I walked to the bathroom and looked at myself in the mirror. I was a single woman flop artist. I'd gained fifteen pounds since I'd quit my job. I felt brain dead.

I knew I had to get back in shape physically, mentally, and professionally. On the white message board next to the front door I wrote five lines in bold, black marker:

Five Miles, Five Days a Week

Five Glasses of Water

Five Articles to Read a Day

Five Projects Completed

Five Kisses

It was my prescription for my new career and my new life. I would ride my exercise bike five miles a day, Monday through Friday.

I would drink at least five glasses of water a day to flush out all the high-carb foods I'd been eating to help get my body back in shape.

I needed to catch up on reading and turn off the TV. My new promise to myself included reading at least five articles or chapters each day from books geared to my new work-at-home career.

As I hunkered down in my office, I set a goal of completing at least five small work-related projects each week. One a day. Who couldn't do that?

Instead of eating twenty or thirty malted milk balls, handfuls of Raisinets, or dozens of Hershey Kisses a day, I'd limit myself to five a day.

I even started dressing for work. My new routine consisted of breakfast, reading and finishing my second cup of tea by 9 AM, riding my exercise bike at least five miles a day, showering, getting dressed (no pajamas allowed at work!), and being on the job in my office by 10 AM each weekday morning.

I still had time for a chocolate-filled treasure hunt with Andrew every once in a while, but my five-step plan taught me that I had a lot more to share with him when he came in the door at 4 PM than silly treasure hunt clues.

My own treasure hunt for a more structured, more successful, work-at-home atmosphere has reaped many rewards in the years that followed. But the best part of all is the knowledge that *who I am* is truly based on *what I do* with the talent God has given me.

These days I use chocolate as a sweet little reward, not as a substitute for work. It's a good plan.

Patricia Lorenz

Candy Kisses

Forget love . . . I'd rather fall in chocolate!

Author Unknown

B ack in the dark ages when I turned eleven in Ms. Daisy Blogg's classroom, the most wonderful thing happened: I fell in love. It was magical as Buddy O'Toole and I zinged whimsical grins across four rows of sixth-grade desks. I was tall for my age and just about as gangly as they come, while Buddy was short and just about as round as they come. But it hardly mattered, for nearly all the boys were shorter than the girls. My mother assured me I was experiencing "puppy love" and that Buddy was just slow shedding his baby fat.

Memories of chocolates and surprises beset my every thought as Valentine's Day drew near. Mother always said that there are chocolates, and then there are chocolates, meaning that few are the Rolls-Royce of good candy. Dad haunted the finest specialty shop in town for the best imported chocolate of the day. Heart-shaped red velvet boxes topped with satiny white bows contained layers of unique hand-dipped varieties. And if one should forage between the nuts and chews, she might find a lovely pair of fourteen-karat earrings. Ah, yes, my dad really knew how to melt her heart, while mother set an elegant Valentine's Day table with Dad's favorites and gifts at each plate.

I could barely wait to hear what our teacher had planned as our tall classroom windows glittered with familiar sweet red angels and assorted hearts. Would we cut and paste tiresome construction paper, add bits of ribbon over paper lace doilies, and exchange the results? Gladly, no. We had made that big step from childhood to upperclassmen and could create our own valentines at home or purchase them at the local five-and-dime.

"Please bring a decorated container with your name clearly marked on the outside," announced Ms. Blogg. "You will make enough valentines for every box." How familiar that sounded as I pondered two scruffy and cantankerous boys who still dipped pigtails in inkwells despite the principal's wrath. And, of course, equality prevailed to include our class's haughty and mean-spirited girl.

While the ladies fancied valentine greetings, the sixth-grade boys were not as sold on the custom, suddenly all too juvenile, silly, and mushy. Regardless, Buddy told me to make sure my container was at least as big as a shoe box because he had been working on an idea. 'Twould be my first experience on cloud nine.

Walking to school, none of us escaped the cloudburst and squall swirling about the playground as we and our valentine treasures ran for cover. The swings and trapezes banged and twirled, ensnarling their chains around and around, then a sudden lull while they untangled at breakneck speed.

After placing our wet boxes on the window sills above

the radiators, we spent the morning glancing at the wrinkled and fading coverings. Ribbons and string hung in limp shambles, making strange arrays of bleeding pigments and hues upon all they touched. Nonetheless, for the girls the day dragged endlessly as we contemplated the party and sharing of our treasures.

As Ms. Blogg read the history of Valentine's Day aloud, a sudden *psst, psst, psst* emanated from the radiator. The class broke out in giggles as we watched chocolate drip, drip, dripping from a corner of the big red shoe box marked "Kathleen." I glanced over at Buddy, but there were no smiles or giggles, just horror written all over his face. He had spent his allowance on the newest Hershey's sensation, foil-wrapped chocolate Kisses, each pasted meticulously upon a sensational card.

The welcomed three o'clock bell rang and the class gathered their valentines under their coats for the drizzly trek home. I caught up with Buddy in the hallway and asked him to meet me across the street at the library. After choosing a corner spot, I set the table with his lovely chocolate-covered card and the knurly candy Kisses. We sat and talked until a grin crossed Buddy's chubby cheeks, then finished off the remains of a valentine box neither of us ever forgot.

Kathe Campbell

Say It with Chocolate

As with most fine things, chocolate has its
season . . . any month whose name
contains the letter A, E, or U is the proper
time for chocolate.

Sandra Boynton

"Hey, honey, do you need hot chocolate, or do you still have some?" Tom asked, the sounds of Wal-Mart beeping noisily in the background.

I hesitated for a second, a little confused. This was probably the first time in six years of marriage that he had ever asked me this question. His usual response to my weekly "Oh, I need to pick up more hot chocolate" was an exaggerated roll of the eye that meant something along the lines of "There goes the chocoholic again. Can't live one day without her fix." So to have him ask me if I needed more was a little bit of a shock.

"No, I'm fine. I just bought that big tub a few days ago."

"Okay. Just wanted to make sure. Didn't want you to run out or anything," he said, teasing me a little.

"I know I'm bad, but I'm not that bad!" I replied. "Even I can't go through that much hot chocolate in three days!"

He just laughed. "Okay. I'll be home in a minute. 'Bye!"

I hung up the phone, shaking my head a little. Inspiration finally struck. My birthday was a few days away. He was probably just trying to be sweet and make sure I had everything I wanted to make my day perfect. I smiled. He was definitely learning.

It's not really his fault. His family, although very loving, just doesn't do holidays, at least not the way my family does. My family jumps on any excuse for a party . . . and chocolate consumption. For Valentine's Day, my sister and I would make a big, heart-shaped cake, chocolate, with red icing. For Saint Patrick's Day, my mom would make corned beef and cabbage . . . and a big chocolate cake, green icing. And these were just the little holidays. Fourth of July, Halloween, Thanksgiving, Christmas, and especially birthdays were huge, blown-out affairs, and usually with my mom's special triple layer, homemade, totally from scratch "Pollyanna" cake—so named because it looked like the huge cakes in the movie of that name, only all chocolate!

My obsession is something Tom just does not understand. He is the type of person who buys a candy bar, takes one bite and leaves it in the fridge for a month. He likes chocolate cream pie, but he'll eat one piece and leave the rest of the pie to rot. He doesn't even like chocolate chip cookies or chocolate cake and refuses to eat either one. How we ever got together is beyond me. He sees my love of chocolate as some kind of defect. So to have him ask me if I needed more hot chocolate was, to say the least, a little surprising.

My birthday arrived and Tom came home from work

proudly carrying a package in his hands. Nothing prepared me for what I was about to open. I removed the paper and I merely stared. It was a thing of beauty, something I never dreamed existed. My eyes teared, and I looked with absolute adoration at the most wonderful man on the planet. He had given me a hot chocolate maker!

For years, every time we'd go into a hotel room, I'd rant about how the hoteliers were discriminating against the chocolate lover. There was always a coffee maker on the counter. Couldn't they throw a few packets of instant hot cocoa in the basket? How hard would that be? For years he had watched me make hot chocolate in the microwave, grumbling under my breath every time I had to reheat water to make more if I wanted seconds (if?). He teased me, rolled his eyes, and tried his hardest to ignore me, but he remembered just how much I loved my hot chocolate. I think it was the first present he had ever bought for me that I didn't know about, or I should say, tell him about, ahead of time. And he had chosen the most perfect present in the world.

To this day, that hot chocolate maker has remained my favorite present out of everything he has ever given me. He's done many sweet things for me, given me many wonderful gifts, but that year, he did the best thing in the world. He said it with chocolate.

Michelle McLean

Eco-friendly Beans

Today, two-thirds of the world's cocoa is produced in Africa, but until oil was discovered, cocoa was Venezuela's number one export.

Along the country's Caribbean coastline and around the shores of Lake Maracaibo, many Venezuelan cacao producers have recently seen a resurgence in demand since they switched to organic farming techniques.

Today, their beans are now preferred by many chocolate gourmets. Organic cacao beans fetch up to four times as much as other beans, which helps compensate the growers for their labor-intensive work. Experts place a high value on Venezuela's single-bean varieties, which produce a cocoa that is purer and more aromatic.

Finger-Lickin' Good!

*Chocolate makes everyone smile
—even bankers.*

Chocolatier Benneville Strohecker

T he moment I saw that brownie mix box in the kitchen cabinet, I fell wholly and madly in love. Brownies! Does anything in this whole wide world smell as good, or taste as scrumptious, as fresh-baked, chocolate-loaded brownies?

For years I had adored the wonderful brownies my beloved Grandma Elsie made. She wasn't around to make some right then. But all the directions to bake real, genuine brownies were right on the back of that box. Why, they would be the simplest thing in the world to make, even for a ten-year-old like me. Wouldn't Mom, Dad, and Grandma Elsie be thrilled?

Climbing up on a chair, I stood on tiptoe to reach the box on the top shelf. Once I had it down on the counter, I carefully read the illustrated instructions. Piece o' cake! One measuring cup, mixing bowl, baking pan, and egg coming up!

Tearing off the top of the box, I ripped open the bag inside and poured its fragrant brown contents into the bowl. Then I cracked the egg and added its shiny contents. Last of all, I carefully measured two-thirds of a cup of water and poured it in. Was I ever proud to know fractions!

The next instruction was "mix well by hand." So I carefully rescrubbed my hands and began beating the mixture with my right hand as I held the bowl firmly with my left one. Over and over I beat the dough, counting the strokes, becoming more and more excited all the time. I could hardly wait until I reached 100 strokes and could pour it all into the waiting pan!

Just then, "Victoria Jean DeNisi!" my father roared. "What in the Sam Hill do you think you're doing?"

I grinned. "Making brownies."

"B-but what are you doing with your hands?"

I nodded toward the directions on the back of the box. "Mixing everything, of course. You know, like it says, 'Mix well by hand.'" Suddenly I looked at my hands and then at his face. Whoops. "Is something wrong?"

At that, he began roaring with laughter. "Honey," he cried, opening a drawer and pulling out a large wooden spoon, "you're not supposed to use your bare hands. You're supposed to use this!"

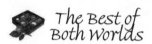

The Best of Both Worlds

One comprehensive scientific study came to the conclusion that for most people, eating chocolate produces both an anticipatory pleasure and a consummatory pleasure. It is an indulgence rather than an addiction. Fifteen percent of men and 40 percent of women admit to having chocolate cravings, and most chocolate cravings occur in late afternoon or early evening.

"Oh." I stared at the wooden spoon and then at my hands, absolutely covered with rich, brown dough. "Then how am I supposed to get this stuff off?"

He grinned and winked. "Lick it off, I suppose. What do you think?"

Sounded good to me. So I did. And so I've done ever since. Why, now I figure half the fun of baking brownies is getting to lick the mixing spoon afterward—as long as no one can see me, of course!

Ummm! Chocolate! Finger-lickin' good. Almost as tasty as the brownies themselves!

Victoria J. Hanson
As told to Bonnie Compton Hanson

chocolate Shake and chocolate cake

Chemically speaking, chocolate really is the world's perfect food.

Michael Levine,
Nutrition Researcher

"Did you hear on the news chocolate is now good for us?" my sister, Faith, said. The buzz went through my friends and family. Chocolate, the dark, rich, decadent stuff we craved, was good for us after all. I called Dad, who was the resident chocolate connoisseur in our family.

"Dad, chocolate is good for us!" I yelled into the phone because Dad's response usually was "What?" until you yelled, and then he'd ask, "Why are you yelling?"

"So?" He heard me this time. "I don't care. I'll eat it anyway."

At eighty-five, Dad had problems with his lungs and heart, and while he did take the doctor's advice on medication and exercise, he ate what he wanted. The man lived for three meals a day and snacks. And those snacks were chocolate: chocolate candy bars, chocolate pudding cups, chocolate ice cream, or various other chocolate delights.

Faith and I ran Dad's errands, did his weekly shopping, and tried to get Dad everything he wanted. He'd been sick, in and out of the hospital for months, with back-to-back infections and pneumonia. So if Dad wanted something to eat like a meatball sandwich, ice cream, or a doughnut, Faith and I ran to get it. But mostly Dad wanted chocolate. One time while Dad was in the hospital, Faith and I were on a chocolate run. We met Dad's doctor in the elevator as we were returning with the goods.

"Doctor, is it all right if Dad eats chocolate?" Faith opened the bag and showed the doctor the chocolate candy bars we had bought.

"Sure, let him have what he wants," the doctor said. "I buy the big boxes of chocolate from the warehouse store. You girls should get your dad a big box."

Evidently there was a chocolate epidemic and the doctor had come down with it, too.

We continued to buy our dad all the chocolate he wanted, whether in or out of the hospital. He never fully recovered from those back-to-back infections, and with another infection, it was back to the hospital. This would be his final stay. Within a week, his lungs began shutting down. He was told on a Monday that he was dying; on Tuesday he called friends to say good-bye. Faith and I spent that final week with him. He was fine with dying. Our mother had passed away twenty-eight years earlier. For the last two weeks, Mom had visited Dad in his dreams, telling him everything would be all right. Wednesday night we asked Dad what he wanted for dinner. He wanted two things: a chocolate shake and a piece of chocolate cake. The woman in the hospital cafeteria made the chocolate shake special for Dad. My sister and I fed him when the food arrived. Dad tried to hold the shake in his trembling hands, but he kept spilling it. He laughed each time it spilled and asked, "Joyce, why are you spilling my shake?" That was Dad's last meal. He died the next morning in his sleep, a happy man. And he is probably eating chocolate right now in heaven.

Joyce Tres

Chocolate Bunnies

Chocolate causes certain endocrine glands
to secrete hormones that affect your feelings and behavior by making you happy. So,
eat lots of chocolate!

Elaine Sherman

I n the center of the kitchen table, the box stood
looking like an artist's pallet swirled with pastels.
An oversize envelope propped up against it had
the word *Sugar* written on the front in tiny, uneven letters.
I picked up the envelope and behind it a chocolate bunny
stared at me through a cellophane window. My heart sang
at the words of love etched throughout the card, and I ran
laughing into the bedroom, where my husband was opening his card and admiring his chocolate bunny. We hid our
bunnies side-by-side in the bedroom, like a deep secret,
behind closed doors and away from visiting guests. That
tradition started our first Easter together as husband and
wife. Thirty-seven years, seventy-four bunnies later,
things haven't changed.

In the early years, we snuggled together in front of the
TV before I disappeared into the kitchen to sacrifice my
bunny first. With a sharp knife, I shaved a reasonable

portion of chocolate and divided it into pieces as close to the same size as possible. I allowed myself a bite or two, or maybe more—my memory is a bit fuzzy on that—before offering the platter to my spouse. He took one piece and said," I don't want any more."

I whispered a prayer of thanks and joyfully nibbled away at the rest until it was gone. He pretended not to notice that night and the following evenings when I repeated the ritual until the bunny had disappeared. Sadly, I licked the chocolate flecks from the foil leaves and presented the blue and yellow candy eyeballs to our dog.

My husband's bunny remained in its colorful box. "When are you going to open your bunny?" I asked.

"That chocolate is driving you crazy," he said, grinning from ear to ear.

Without my help, I decided, he would never open his bunny, so I lopped off his head (the bunny's), stuffed it in a sandwich bag, and put it in his lunchbox. He came home that night and said, "Don't put a bunny's head in my lunch again. The guys at work will never let me live this one down."

After that incident, I prepared his bunny the same way I handled mine. I was fair about it, starting with my bunny the day after Easter and saving his until the next week.

About the tenth year of our marriage, I decided to wait and see how long my husband would keep his bunny. One year later, I took matters into my own hands and shed real tears at having to throw away an elderly chocolate rabbit. I vowed, right then and there, never to waste another bunny.

At the next Easter, I made sure to purchase a foil-wrapped bunny for my beloved and thought of new possibilities. The Monday after Easter, we consumed my bunny. Perhaps I am exaggerating when I say "we."

I started early in the morning, biting off the bunny's ears and promising myself to save the rest for a later time. Around midday I slipped the bunny from the box, snapped off his hollow head and crammed it into my mouth. My husband walked through the kitchen and glanced at my chipmunk cheeks.

"Want a piece of chocolate?" I mumbled around the crunchy yellow and blue eyeballs.

He shook his head and laughed. "Can't leave that alone, can you?" he said.

I could if I wanted to, I thought, ripping off the foil leaves and licking at the flecks of chocolate.

The bunny was gone before sunset.

My husband's bunny sat on the dresser day after day. I was determined not to bother it if he ate it within the month. But the day came when I could stand it no longer. With a light touch, I opened the bottom of the bunny box and pulled out the folded white shelf upon which it rested. Somehow those tricky marketers had the bunny suspended in a hole cut in the plaid cardboard. I wiggled and twisted the foil bunny, but he resisted my efforts. With a pair of scissors, I slit the cardboard and pulled out the bunny, my mouth watering at the scent of chocolate. I unwrapped his lower extremities and bit off his feet. With great care, I rewrapped the bunny and put him back in the box. That night my husband didn't even glance at the bunny on the dresser.

In the days that followed, I repeated the process, going from knees to tummy to chest and to neck. I congratulated myself on my ingenious plan, until the day my husband stopped in front of the dresser and said, "Why is my bunny so short?"

What could I say? "He shrank." "He was defective." "He melted." It didn't matter what I said because my husband wasn't listening. He was ripping open the box and laughing so hard.

It really made me mad.

But then he tore off the foil wrapper and handed me the chocolate head—and I forgave him. Who could hold a grudge against a spouse offering you his last bite of chocolate?

The path to an enduring relationship is built on love and forgiveness, but a bit of chocolate along the way sweetens the journey.

Linda Kaullen Perkins

A Spoonful of Fudge

**There's nothing better than a good friend,
except a good friend with chocolate.**

Linda Grayson

Spiral back in time with me to a mid-December day in 1947 to one of my treasured memories.

With our teacher's guidance, my third-grade class planned the Christmas party held on our final day before the holiday break. Our classroom already looked festive thanks to a live Christmas tree decorated with our artwork. Cut-out paper snowflakes adorned the tall windows, and in free time we'd made construction paper chains, which we used to decorate every available space in the room.

But now the most important part of getting ready was upon us. Miss Marshak asked for volunteers to bring Christmas napkins, cookies, and punch.

"Now, what else would be good to have at the party?" she asked.

A boy in the last row hollered, "Fudge!"

At his one-word answer, I sat up straight and waved my hand in the air. When Miss Marshak did not call on me immediately, I bounced up and down in my chair and gestured furiously.

"Yes, Nancy," she finally said.

"I'll bring the fudge. My mother makes the best fudge in the world." My mouth watered at the thought of the creamy, rich chocolate candy my entire family loved.

I could hardly wait to get home and tell my mother that I'd volunteered to bring fudge for the party. She'd be so excited to share her special fudge with all my classmates. I barely felt the cold December air as I hurried along the six blocks from school to our apartment building. My feet scarcely touched the stairs as I sailed up the three flights to our door.

Mother stopped peeling potatoes when I burst into the kitchen. I announced the great news, but I didn't get the reaction I'd expected. Her face paled. "Fudge? Isn't there something else you can bring?"

"No. Other people signed up for the rest." My excitement deflated like a pricked balloon.

What could be wrong?

Mother shrugged, picked up the potato peeler, and said, "It's all right. I'll make the fudge."

The December days slid by, one by one. I helped Mother put up our Christmas decorations. Dad took my brothers and me to pick out a tree, and Mother spent her days wrapping packages and baking special cookies and Christmas cakes. At school we practiced for our part in the all-school musical program, read Christmas stories in reading time, and created our own in Language Arts period. Giggles got louder as Christmas surrounded us.

Finally, the day before the party arrived. Our teacher went over a checklist to make sure everyone remembered what they were to bring the next day. How could I forget? I'd thought every day about the wonderful chocolaty fudge Mother would make. I could almost taste its smoothness and the lingering sweetness it left.

When I got home that afternoon, my baby brother was crying, and Mother looked about to cry along with him. "What's wrong?" I asked. My worry centered not on the baby or my mother, but on the fudge.

Mother sank into a kitchen chair. "I've made three batches of fudge today, and none of them worked. They're all too soft. I can't send it to school."

I had no idea why she was so disturbed. Fudge was always soft and gooey. We spooned it up every time we had it. "Why?" was all I could think to say.

"Nancy," my mother said, "fudge is not meant to be eaten with a spoon. It should be firm enough to pick it up in a piece and pop into your mouth. I beat and beat it, but it's like it always is when I make it. Too soft. And I made it three times today!"

Tears welled in her eyes, and my baby brother reached up and patted her cheek. Maybe even he knew how bad she felt. How could I bring the fudge to school? I loved my mother's fudge, but

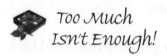

Too Much Isn't Enough!

The Swiss consume more chocolate per capita than any other country, on average twenty-two pounds of chocolate each year; Americans consume eleven pounds. The British fall in between with an average of seventeen pounds of chocolate (or about 180 bars) per person per year. They actually spend more money on chocolate than on fruits and vegetables combined.

maybe nobody else would. Maybe they'd laugh when they saw it. I worked up my courage and asked, "What are we going to do?"

The next morning, I carried a big pan of fudge and twenty-one spoons to school.

The soft candy was the hit of the party. After we had our punch and cookies, everyone gathered around the cake pan of fudge, spoon in hand, and dug in. My fears were never realized. One of the boys licked his spoon and said, "You were right. Your mom does make the best fudge in the world." Echoes of agreement sounded around the circle. We dipped our spoons for more.

Some years later, Mother began to make a new fudge recipe that contained marshmallow crème. The ads promised it was foolproof—firm fudge every time. They were right, but the spoonfuls of soft fudge we'd eaten all those years before remained my favorite.

Nancy Julien Kopp

The Chocoholic Grandma

The best way to get two pounds
of chocolate home from the store
in a hot car is to eat it in the parking lot.

Author Unknown

When I first met my husband's grandma, the first thing I noticed was she seemed to like chocolate more than I did. Perhaps it was the way Grandma hid her chocolate cravings from the rest of us and kept her stash to herself. When someone gave Grandma a present of chocolate, she'd excuse herself and hide her loot.

Later when my two young sons asked if they could have some of her chocolate, she usually responded that she forgot where she put the golden egg.

"Grandma's getting old and forgets where she puts things," she'd say. "After you kids leave I'll probably remember what I did with the chocolate and then you can have some next time you come for a visit."

There was never a next time. The children would always remember to ask on their next visit, and every time she had no idea where she had left her chocolate. What kind of Grandma doesn't share the chocolate with kids?

Grandma refused to get a housekeeper; she was afraid

they were only after her chocolate. We encouraged Grandma to start her own local chocoholic support group, a place where she could get help with other women her age who loved chocolate. She was always reluctant. "Why at my age do I need to stop eating chocolate? It's the only thing I have left in life."

So we stopped harassing Grandma about her addiction and started to learn to live with Grandma's dependency on the cocoa bean, as we were constantly reminded, "It's better to eat chocolate than to drink whiskey."

Every year we would ask, "Grandma, what do you want for Christmas?"

"Well, I'm not sure if you know how much I like chocolate, but a little chocolate would be nice and the darker the better. Of course, it's not good for me, so I don't need much."

Year after year Grandma would open one present after another. There were dark chocolate mints, dark chocolate caramels, dark chocolate truffles, dark chocolate strawberries, and dark chocolate-covered peanuts. As soon as she had opened the last gift, with a blink of her eye and a nod from her nose, those presents disappeared like Santa's eight tiny reindeer.

Grandma is turning ninety next year and we're planning the celebration. I've already suggested that we have chocolate cake, chocolate ice cream, chocolate pie, chocolate soufflé, chocolate pretzels, chocolate-chip cookies, chocolate flowers, chocolate balloons, and drink hot chocolate. That much chocolate will probably make most of us sick, however.

Best If Used By

Stale chocolate develops a chalky-white sheen. Commercial chocolate has a shelf life of about eight weeks, while high-quality specialty chocolates taste best if eaten within two weeks.

So we asked Grandma what she wants for her ninetieth birthday, and she replied, "It would be nice to go on a cruise. I hear that you can eat all you want, whenever you want, and my friend Mabel says they have the best chocolate desserts she's ever eaten."

We've made a deal with Grandma: if she shares the chocolates that she received this year for Christmas, we'll send her on a cruise for her birthday. I say let her eat her chocolate and have her chocolate cake on the cruise, too. After all, if it weren't for her, none of us would be here enjoying our own chocolate addictions.

L. J. Martin

Somebody's Sweetheart

Stress wouldn't be so hard to take
if it were chocolate covered.

Author Unknown

V alentine's Day was just around the corner, and my feelings of dread were already beginning to mount. For the last three years the Tri Hi Y girls organization at my high school held a fund-raiser, "Select Your Southern Sweetheart," where boyfriends and dads were encouraged to purchase big red hearts full of chocolate candy for their "sweethearts." I was way too shy and retiring to have a boyfriend, and I hadn't lived with my dad since I was five, so there would be no chocolate-filled red heart on my desk in homeroom class this year—again. At that time only a handful of kids in the whole school lived in divorced homes. On days like this, I felt different—like the little girl with her face pressed up against the glass, always on the outside looking in.

I could count on my mom not recognizing Valentine's Day. Raising four kids alone and working to make ends meet, she barely had time to acknowledge Christmas. "Wrap up that shirt I bought you last week and put it under the tree for yourself," she directed before she headed out to work. She was humorless and angry most of the time. So I shouldn't have been surprised on that bleak day in winter when she announced during one of her many mother meltdowns that she was done with this motherhood gig. "You need to call your dad to come and get you. It's his turn," she barked. Still I was totally surprised. I did all I could to help her, handling dinner, dishes, laundry; I even did windows.

Nonetheless, she was done. So one minute I was living in Tennessee with a handful of good friends, and the next I was in North Carolina with a dad I hardly knew and a stepmom and sister I had barely met. My world would have rocked out of control, but my dad wouldn't let it. Every night at the dinner table he kicked into what the family came to call "Daddy's Dinner Time Shtick." I would laugh at his jokes and antics until sweet tea nearly sprayed out of my nose! The laughter and love made the transition bearable.

Not long after I moved in, I stopped by the store to pick up something for my stepmother. All of the candy on display made me realize Valentine's Day was approaching. I'd been so busy adjusting to a new high school and unfamiliar surroundings that I hadn't remembered it. I took some comfort in the fact that at the new school I wouldn't be the only girl in homeroom without a red cardboard heart full of chocolate on her desk.

When I walked into the house, my little sister, Ren, was standing in the doorway of my room pointing toward the bed. Piled on top of the pillow was a mountain of assorted chocolates and a note that read "Happy Valentine's Day from the Legendary Chicken Fairy" written in my dad's handwriting. "I got some, too," Ren smiled. My dad offered a hilarious explanation for his alter ego: Santa Claus comes at Christmas, the Easter Bunny hands out eggs— somebody's got to take care of business on Valentine's Day.

After laughing until I cried, I sat down on the bed next to a pile of foil-wrapped chocolate and the card that still had me grinning. Then it dawned on me—I no longer felt like the little girl with her face impaled on the glass looking inside and wanting desperately to be allowed in. I belonged; I was somebody's sweetheart.

Seven months later, I was off to college in California. When Valentine's Day approached, I found a package in the mail—a box of chocolates and a card with the return address: from Legendary Chicken Fairy. I sent my dad a valentine with the same name in the return address. We carried on like that every Valentine's Day for decades.

My dad passed away last September. The days come and go and I miss the laughter. The entire family does.

Valentine's Day rolled around and my youngest daughter, Ashley, was home from college for the weekend. I walked into my bedroom and there on my pillow was a pile of chocolates and a note that read "Happy Valentine's Day from the Legendary Chicken Fairy" written in Ashley's handwriting. How proud my dad would be that the legend, the love—and the chocolate—would live on!

Linda Newton

Accomplices in chocolate

If you get melted chocolate all over
your hands, you're eating it too slowly.

Author Unknown

The first time it happened was on a sunny fall afternoon in the year 1964. My almost-eight-year-old sister, Annette, and I were busy raking leaves into a gigantic pile directly in front of the swing set. Just as we were about to set down our rakes and hit the swings, our mom called us into the house. As usual, we were just a bit reluctant, never knowing whether we were headed for trouble or for a plate of freshly baked cookies.

This day was a milestone.

"I need you girls to go to the store for me," Mom said. She needed macaroni, two cans of vegetable soup, and one can of corn for that evening's supper.

"Barbie, you are in charge of the money," she said as she handed me a five-dollar bill.

We hopped on our bicycles and were off on a new mission. Two and a half blocks and two and a half minutes later, we parked our bikes and went shopping.

Annette and I collected the items on our mental list as

the clerk waited at the register. We slid the four items onto the counter.

Then came my little sister's quandary. What is a child to do when, for the first time, there is no parent around when the child wants to beg, "Can I have?" or "Can we get?" Well, of course, pointing at the Hershey's bar from the vast selection of temptation right in front of her face, she looked to her older sister. Being almost ten and much wiser, I instantly responded to her wanting eyes.

"Get me one, too," I whispered, and as she grabbed for it, "No, a Crunch bar."

As our little hearts pounded, the lady rang up our purchases and placed them in a bag.

I stuffed the change into my jacket pocket and zipped it up. Then, with the bag securely set in my bike basket, we rode around the corner and out of the clerk's sight. Once safely stopped, I reached into the bag and handed Annette her Hershey's bar. We stuffed the wrappers into our pants pockets and proceeded on our bikes, casually eating our chocolate. We rode so slowly toward home that it was difficult keeping our bikes upright. Three houses from home, we had both finished eating and we needed to stop. Instinctively, we showed each other our teeth, checked our jackets for crumbs, and looked for any other telltale sign of our little misdeed.

Proudly, we handed Mom the bag and the change. We returned her approving smile with our own big—and just in case—closed-lip smiles. The matter of the receipt didn't seem to concern us. Perhaps because we knew our mom was not like our grandmother, who matched each and every item to a price on the receipt to make sure she wasn't overcharged.

Yes, this day had been a milestone, and I don't think chocolate had ever been so gratifying. As with many a first-time experience, an individual will often keep trying to recapture that initial exhilarating rush.

From that day on, our mom trusted us with a short shopping list and a five-dollar bill at least once weekly.

By winter, we had our method of operation down pat. In fact, winter was the perfect setup. Having to walk gave us more time to savor our chocolate and we could wash away any evidence with snow.

Sometimes, chilling our chocolate in the snow provided us with just enough diversion from our usual scheme. Other times we'd challenge ourselves. Maybe in the checkout lane I'd say out loud to Annette, "Mom wants a Nut Goodie." Double genius! This little comment threw the clerk off (lest she be onto us) *and* we got to share another candy bar to boot.

Through the months, our mom's confidence in us increased. It pleased her to see how eager we were to help save her time in her day-to-day tasks.

Then it was April, early spring, when again we could use our bikes. This day, Mom handed me a thick wad of ones, along with a written list, because this time there were too many items to memorize. The list read: one pound bologna, one head lettuce, one loaf white bread, one jar salad dressing, two cans tomato soup, one box soda crackers, one Hershey's bar, one Nestle Crunch, and one Nut Goodie.

Barbara Paulson

In Emergency, Break Glass

The twelve-step chocoholics program:
Never be more than twelve steps away
from chocolate!

Terry Moore

"F inally! You're home!" I scoffed at my husband, arriving from work, walking toward our front door. "I've barely survived being stuck here for almost three days by myself with these sick kids." Just as he was about to step into the house, I grabbed a fistful of my husband's railroad bibs from his lumpy chest pocket, leaned close, lowered my voice to my most threatening tone, and demanded through clenched teeth, "I need some chocolate and I need it now."

Trying to hide a smirk, my unruffled husband answered, "I've got some hidden away just for such an emergency."

"What? There's been some in the house all this time?" Rather than be thankful he had thought ahead, I was irritated I'd gone without it needlessly. My easygoing husband didn't argue with me, though. He simply set his duffle bag down in the foyer and disappeared into our bedroom to find the chocolate, hoping, as always, the confection would calm the snarling beast that used to be his wife.

"It's in the bedroom?" I asked, following him.

"Obviously your nose isn't working as well as it usually does," he snickered as he handed me the candy bar.

He checked on our ailing kids, gently stroking their foreheads and commiserating with them for not only suffering from the flu, but also being cooped up with grumpy Mom, while I ripped into the long-awaited, melt-in-your-mouth milk chocolate with creamy nougat and peanuts. *Aah.*

How did he know I'd crave chocolate? The need did seem to reoccur with regularity every twenty-eight days, but why was I so dependent on chocolate to get me through an emotional phase? Is this a character flaw I was doomed to live with?

Historians inform us our stout ancestors survived extended periods of famine precisely because they were able to live out the lean times with their cushion of survival already in place. Is this craving part of a deep genetic survival mode? The natural way each successive generation survives?

As our four boys grew older, my husband jokingly taught them the wisdom he had learned through the years. With a gleam in his eyes and flamboyant passion in his voice, he advised, "Boys, you take a piece of chocolate, put it inside a glass box, and hang it on the wall in your bedroom. In an emergency, when you hear snarling and growling on the other side of your rattling bedroom door, break the glass and slip the chocolate under the door; when you hear the shredding of the wrapper, open the door and run for your life!"

Hmm. If he wasn't so right, I'd be offended.

I've tried to wean my addiction to milk chocolate filled with creamy caramel and dark chocolate dipped in crunchy peanut butter, really I have. If I can't have one of my favorites, it's not worth the calories consumed. See— I'm making progress.

Through it all, my husband and I have modeled for our children what true marriage is really like. It's not our job to change the harmless habits or character flaws of each other; it's our job to love each other just as we are, grumpy or happy, with cushion or without.

While visiting my oldest son and his wife recently, my very pregnant daughter-in-law called out as my son headed for the door to do errands, "I need some chocolate!"

"Any particular kind?" he asked patiently.

See—he learned well. His generation is going to survive too.

Sandy McKeown

The Mickey Capers

Researchers have discovered that chocolate
produced some of the same reactions in the
brain as marijuana. The researchers also discovered other similarities between the two,
but can't remember what they are.

Matt Lauer, NBC's Today Show

M y dear friend Betsy's mother, Mickey, an octoge-
narian, is obviously the person most responsible
for Betsy's outrageous sense of humor . . . one of
the main reasons Betsy and I have been friends since 1981.
I'm not sure if my fondness for Mickey is because she has
a devilish twinkle in her eye every time she comes to visit
from the East or because my own mother died years earlier at age fifty-seven, and I think of Mickey as a sort of
mother figure. Whatever it is, for some reason as our
friendship grew, I decided to start a "gotcha gift" exchange
with my favorite surrogate mother many years ago.

Over the years Mickey and I have gift-wrapped the
dumbest stuff you could imagine, oddball items found
mainly at yard sales and pawned off on each other
admidst merriment and mayhem, mostly during the
Christmas holidays or birthdays.

One Christmas I stopped at Betsy's house to see Mickey during her annual holiday visit and to deposit her annual "gotcha gift" under Betsy's tree. If I remember correctly, it was a horrible T-shirt I'd fashioned from some red and black knitted afghan squares I'd found at a rummage sale. And, like always, there was a gift for me from Mickey under the tree.

I couldn't wait to see what that year's worthless, goofy gift would be. When the time came for me to open mine, I was shocked to discover not a gag gift, but instead a box of Whitman's chocolates, the big box, two layers tall.

"Mickey!" I shouted, "You're not supposed to get me a real gift, you know that. What did you do this for? I got you something stupid, as always. Honestly, you shouldn't have. But you know how much I love chocolate. So this is very, very sweet of you." I couldn't stop gushing over the first real gift she'd ever given me.

I got up to give her a hug, trying to decide if I should open the box right then and there and share it with everyone in the room, or if I should take it home unopened and savor each delightful piece of my

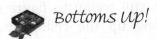

Bottoms Up!

People have been drinking chocolate in liquid form for 3,000 years. In the 1500s the Aztec emperor Montezuma introduced the Spanish conquistador Cortez to his favorite drink, hot chocolate, which he drank from solid gold goblets.

Today, many Europeans, especially the Spanish, drink hot chocolate for breakfast instead of coffee. But don't confuse hot chocolate and hot cocoa. They are two different drinks. Hot chocolate is made from melted chocolate and hot cocoa is made from cocoa powder.

chocolate treasure. Secretly, I was wanting to take it home and pig out by myself. But Betsy, also a chocolate lover, had other ideas.

"Oh, go ahead and open it now," Betsy pleaded. I knew she wanted to dig in with me, so I gave in to save face. As I carefully slid my fingernail under the cellophane wrapper covering the box of chocolates I was secretly hoping that everyone would take just one piece and leave the rest for me. Carefully, I lifted the lid.

I blinked my eyes and stared at the box before me. Mickey had done it again. She'd taken a bite out of every single piece of chocolate in that big box.

"Well," she grinned. "I just wanted to make it easier for you to know what was inside each piece."

I'm still trying to figure out how she did it without messing up the cellophane. I'm also trying to figure out how to get her back for that one.

Patricia Lorenz

A Lifelong Love of Chocolate

There are two kinds of people in the world.
Those who love chocolate, and communists.

Leslie Moak Murray

M y love affair with chocolate began at a tender young age. In elementary school we didn't have many choices when it came to the cafeteria food. We did, however, have a choice between plain milk and chocolate milk. If only the answers to my math tests had come so easily.

Of course, I opted for the little brown-and-white carton. A straw was unnecessary, for once I pried open the cardboard container, the drink was gone in a few gulps. Once the carton was empty, it became the receptacle for all the uneaten food on my lunch tray. On Monday it may have been mystery meatloaf, on Tuesday turnips, Wednesday Waldorf salad, Thursday three-bean salad, on Friday fish sticks.

When I became a Brownie (the nonedible kind), the highlight of my year was the annual Girl Scout Cookie Sale. I devoured the chocolate mint cookies, which at the time sold for a mere fifty cents a box. Too bad there wasn't a merit badge for most cookies eaten. Oh, and how could

I forget those incredible s'mores by the campfire?

Another annual highlight during my childhood was Halloween. You can keep your candy corn. Hand over the M&M's, Raisinets, and Hershey's Kisses. To this day, I rifle through my sons' Halloween bags, masquerading as quality control, confiscating my favorite chocolate confections. It's for their own good, of course.

As I grew, and I mean grew, so did my taste for chocolate. On my honeymoon, the Ghirardelli shop in San Francisco was a must. Want to know the real reason I married my husband? His sister sold Godiva chocolates in her gift stores. Okay, the secret's out.

Throughout my two pregnancies, I was advised to stay away from chocolate. After all, chocolate has caffeine. Yeah, right. I experimented with carob, but I couldn't fool my taste buds. Hey, when a woman is pregnant she's supposed to have cravings. So I craved chocolate. To justify indulging in my cravings, I'd splurge on chocolate yogurt or chocolate ice cream. I figured the benefits of the calcium balanced the negatives of the chocolate. When I nursed my sons, they enjoyed chocolate breast milk.

My favorite holiday? Not Christmas. Not Thanksgiving. The answer is obvious: Valentine's Day. Forget the hearts and flowers and flowery cards. Just give me a heart-shaped box of chocolates. Be still, my heart. Easter comes in a close second with its chocolate Easter bunnies. And, yes, just as I eat my Oreos in a methodical manner, I start with the bunny's ears and work my way down.

My favorite restaurant? A fondue place where they bring you a pot of hot, gooey, yummy chocolate, complete with goodies for dipping, such as fruit, marshmallows, and chunks of pound cake.

My favorite theme park? It's a no-brainer: Hershey Park. They even have a spa where chocolate is a main ingredient of many spa treatments. If you ask me, any chocolate not ingested is wasted chocolate. And Hershey's Times Square is chocoholic heaven. Talk about a kid in a candy store.

Most people go to Vegas to gamble . . . and see Elvis. Not *moi*. I head straight to M&M's World. While others are busy counting their winnings at the slots, I'm busy counting my M&M's.

Then a dream came true. No, I didn't hit the jackpot in Vegas. I landed a job with a marketing agency that had M&M/Mars as a client. Ah, the taste of sweet success. Although it's been years since I worked there, I fondly recall the friendships I formed with Red and Yellow M&M's characters.

Imagine my joy in recent years when health experts revealed the medical benefits of chocolate. Now granted, all these years I'd been partial to milk chocolate. But in the interest of my health, I've expanded my chocolate repertoire to include the dark variety.

In short, my philosophy on life is similar to Forrest Gump's: "Life is like a box of chocolates . . . just keep your hands off mine."

Darcy Silvers

The Chocolate Marauder

I have three good reasons for eating
chocolate: I love it, I love it, I love it.

Patricia Lorenz

I firmly believe that nutritionists who developed the
food pyramid had an almost unforgivable lapse in
judgment when they failed to include chocolate in
their design. Seldom does a day go by when chocolate does
not pass my lips. Quite simply, it is a required staple in my
diet. That being said, I do have discriminating taste; not just
any confection meets my standards. I have been known to
travel great distances in order to obtain the quality chocolate that I crave.

My sister is well aware of my chocolate desires, and for
my birthday one year, she invested in a decadent box of
sweets from an upper-end chocolatier. The lavish metallic-
orange box was festooned with ribbons and an ornate
bow. It was a virtual treasure trove designed exclusively
for a chocolate lover. To ensure the safety of her invest-
ment until my birthday, my sister carefully hid the gift
away on a shelf in her closet. She was determined that no
one—friend, family, or foe—breech its contents.

She soon discovered, however, that I was not the only

member of the family with a taste for expensive chocolate. Unknown to her at the time, Jack was also attracted to rich, dark candies. Despite the fact that my sister had so carefully hidden my box of birthday chocolate deep within the confines of her darkened closet, Jack was well aware of its presence in the house. But he was also very cunning and knew better than to attempt to snatch a single caramel-covered bite while my sister was home. Instead, he patiently waited and carefully plotted his chocolate pilfering strategy.

Finally, the opportunity came. My sister bounced out of the house, jovially calling out to Jack to be good. She reminded him that she would be gone for only a few short minutes. As soon as she shut and locked the front door, he made his move. He slunk up the stairs, entered the room with the stealth of a cat burglar, and pushed against the closet door, which he knew had a tendency not to close tightly. He went straight to the hiding place and pulled the box off of the shelf. He carefully removed the packaging. Laying the ribbon aside without disturbing a single curl, he pried open the box and immediately began gorging himself on the exquisite chocolate candies.

When my sister returned home, she sensed immediately that something was not as it should be with Jack. Perhaps it was the guilty look in his dark, woebegone eyes, or perhaps it was the odor emanating from the chocolate and raspberry jelly stained nose of the ten-pound poodle that gave it away. Whatever the reason, she realized with horror that the dog had discovered the outrageously expensive box of candy.

My sister raced upstairs to her closet, with Jack close to her heels, and gasped at the sight. There before her eyes was a partially emptied box of chocolate. Neither the box nor the ribbon had the slightest scratch or bite mark. The same could not be said of the chocolate.

Of course, my sister's first concern was the health of her beloved but rotten poodle. A call to the vet provided her with the assurance that, despite his antics, Jack would almost certainly be fine. After several nervous hours carefully observing his behavior, it was obvious that the dog would indeed suffer no ill effects from his chocolate thievery. With a sigh, my sister dug the credit card from the depths of her wallet and ordered yet another outrageously expensive box of chocolate for me for my birthday. When the shipment arrived, however, she made certain that it was kept in plain sight on a very high shelf in the pantry. It was much safer that way.

Terri Duncan

[EDITORS' NOTE: Keep those chocolates away from prying paws! Chocolate can be harmful to our pets, depending upon their size, health, and other factors, including the amount and type of chocolate ingested. Dogs are extremely sensitive to theobromine, a stimulant in the cacao bean. Watch your pet carefully for signs of distress, and don't hesitate to call your vet if you suspect a problem.]

"I try to eat a varied diet. One day I'll eat dark chocolate, one day I'll eat white chocolate, and one day I'll eat milk chocolate."

Reprinted by permission of Aaron Bacall. ©2006 Aaron Bacallo.

The Revolving Door

Every time I say that word exercise,
I wash my mouth out with chocolate.

Author Unknown

O ne of my most cherished friends is chocolate. Even pronouncing the word makes me salivate. Chocolate has been a pure, constant, and delicious companion since I was a child.

My sisters and I all battle the scale. Sugar is our nemesis. My sister Linda and I have an ongoing joke that we have never been thin at the same time. We are always giving each other pep talks about losing weight. We try to motivate each other without interfering with our beloved chocolate.

One winter morning I got on the scale and wept. How did the number I was staring at happen? I swore that I would start my diet that day and would give up chocolate until I reached my goal. To seemingly guarantee my promise to myself, I called Linda and said it aloud to her. Now it was real and that made it scary.

To my surprise, four weeks passed and I had not cheated once. I worked downtown and decided one day to do some errands. As I was walking down Chicago's main boulevard, I looked up and realized that I was waiting for the traffic light to change in front of a Fannie May Candy Store. This was my second favorite chocolate in the world, next to Cadbury.

As I looked in the window at the display of boxes filled with chocolate butter creams, turtles, and fudge, my knees started to buckle. I almost had to hold on to the side of the building. I could feel my resolve dissolving. "One month," I kept saying to myself. "You have gone without chocolate for one month. Keep walking. Cross the street. Now."

I was not listening. The imagined taste of the chocolate on my tongue had taken over. My brain had disengaged. Only my taste buds were operating in anticipation of what I was about to do. I walked to the store's revolving door and pushed hard to make the door go as fast as it could. As the door swung into the store, I was ready to disembark toward the candy counter.

But I found that I could not stop revolving and could not enter the store. Somehow the door kept going until I was again outside on the street. I looked up in shock to see my sister Linda behind me pushing that door with all her strength. I had pushed myself into the store and she had pushed me out.

Linda happened to be passing by at the moment I weakened. She saw me start my journey toward chocolate and moved as quickly as she could to save me. And she did. We laughed so hard that my need for a chocolate fix passed for the moment. The next craving was an absolute surety. The question was not if, but when, and where would Linda be when I needed her!

Elynne Chaplik-Aleskow

Wanted: A Cold Day in Florida

Nothing chocolate ... nothing gained.

Author Unknown

"Turn the air conditioner down a little colder," I say. We sit in shorts and T-shirts, staring at unending blue skies outside our windows. We live in Florida, where the temperature often hovers around ninety-two degrees. It's the land of swimming pools, flip-flops, and sun-drenched beaches. It's that place where winter means you might think about wearing a sweater. There's no snow here, of course. No icicles. The roads are sizzling. So my children and I turn our air conditioner lower and pretend that it's cold outside.

We do have a reason . . . a good reason, we think. It's about enjoying the simple, good times we have together. It's about home, about being in the kitchen making steaming hot chocolate topped with melting white marshmallows. It's become a family tradition for us—making hot chocolate any month of the year. It's something that brings us together. When hot chocolate is being made, the video game is paused. A book is put down. The computer waits.

My daughter helps me stir milk in a pot on the stove. My son opens a bag of fresh marshmallows. I reach into the cabinet for our three favorite mugs—the big ones. The recipe is simple: three cups of low-fat milk, one-third cup unsweetened cocoa, one-half cup of sugar, and as many marshmallows as you want. We heat the milk, cocoa, and sugar slowly so the mixture doesn't scorch. My daughter talks to me as she stirs, and I silently hope that the milk takes a long time to heat.

As my son pours marshmallows into his mug, he asks, "Is it ready yet?"

"Not quite," I say.

Then he reaches his hand into the marshmallow bag, pops a few into his mouth, and smiles. We watch over the pot on the stove, waiting for our hot chocolate to steam. We stir it constantly, and swirls gradually appear on top. The brew smells wonderfully delicious and decadently chocolaty. Then when all the dots of cocoa have disappeared, we pour our homemade hot chocolate over the marshmallows that line the bottom of each cup. They float to the top to become our first taste of sweetness. Sometimes we drink our hot chocolate in the kitchen. But more often we take our cups into the family room, nestle into the comfy couch and chairs, and just enjoy being together. A little cold air. A lot of hot chocolate. Family time couldn't be sweeter.

J. M. Long

Just Like Grandma's

Equal amounts of dark chocolate and
white chocolate is a balanced diet.

Author Unknown

T hough there's no scientific evidence to back me
up, I'm quite sure the love of chocolate is genetic.
Grandma Pete, Daddy, and I can't make it
through the day without a daily dose of chocolate.

One of our favorite forms for the intake of chocolate is
chocolate crinkles cookies. Not only are they heavenly to
smell as they bake, but it's like biting into a chewy
brownie once they're ready to be eaten.

My mother was never much of a cook, and baking was
totally out of the question, so when it came to learning my
way around the kitchen I had to find another source of
information. When I was thirteen, our family planned to
rent a cabin for a week on a northern Wisconsin lake. It
would be a perfect time to surprise Daddy with a batch of
chocolate crinkle cookies. Grandma Pete wrote down the
recipe. It couldn't be too difficult to follow a recipe, could
it? Since our kitchen at home was void of baking ingredients, Grandma gave me the four squares of unsweetened
chocolate I'd need. The day before our vacation began and

while my parents were at work, I baked. It was a shame opening all the doors and windows to let the chocolate smell escape, but I didn't want to ruin the surprise. I lined a shoebox with aluminum foil and tucked the cookies inside.

With great pride I presented my boxful of cookies to Daddy on our first day of vacation. He was impressed I could tell. "Just like Grandma's," I boasted. "I want you to be the first to try them."

"Umm," he reached out and grabbed two cookies. In the twinkling of an eye and with the first bite of his cookie, the smile he wore turned to a look of shock. "Well, maybe not *just* like Grandma's."

It was my turn to try a cookie. My ego deflated in a huge whoosh. I wasn't sure what to do with the chocolate-coated salty mess inside my mouth. Once I was able to swallow the goo and wash it down with a glass of water, I moaned, "But I followed the recipe."

Mom was enjoying herself. "It's not as easy as it looks, is it? This thing called baking." She laughed all the way down to the dock where her friend Milly was already sunbathing. I was humiliated.

Daddy still held the offending cookie in his hand. Suddenly he dunked it into the coffee mug in front of him. "It's not that bad," he lied. Somehow during the week, Daddy managed to choke down the entire boxful of cookies.

The next time I saw Grandma Pete, we went over the recipe she'd written for me line by line. I learned that in Grandma language a small "t" means teaspoon, not tablespoon, of salt. With the mystery of cookies gone wrong solved, Grandma once again gave me four squares of unsweetened chocolate and encouraged me to try again.

The following week when Daddy came home from work, I said, "Guess what? I baked today." And held out a plate of chocolate crinkles.

An expression of something like panic flickered across his face. He gave me a lopsided grin, got a mugful of coffee, and prepared to dunk. "Try it without dunking," I urged.

He did. A smile as big as his love for me lit up the kitchen as he said, "Just like Grandma's."

I'm not sure if it was Daddy's need for chocolate or a decision to encourage me that gave him strength to eat all my chocolate salt crinkles. But I'm fairly certain that the motivation never to give up is an environmental heritage.

Susan Engebrecht

Chocolate Crinkles

½ cup vegetable oil
4 squares (4 ounces) melted unsweetened chocolate
2 cups granulated sugar
4 eggs
2 teaspoons vanilla
2 cups flour
2 teaspoons baking powder
1 teaspoon salt
1 cup powdered sugar

Preheat oven to 350 degrees.
Mix oil, chocolate, and granulated sugar together.
Blend in one egg at a time until well mixed.
Add vanilla.
Stir flour, baking powder, and salt into oil mixture.
Chill several hours, or overnight.
Roll dough into teaspoon-size balls and then roll in
    powdered sugar.
Place about 2 inches apart on greased baking sheet
    and bake 8–10 minutes.

Susan Engebrecht

Chester and the Chocolate-Covered Cherries

I can give up chocolate anytime I want—
but why?

Mary Englund Murphy

M y favorite uncle, Chester, opened a box of chocolate-covered cherries and said, "Take one. Take as
many as you want."

I couldn't believe my ears. "As many as I want? Really?"

"Sure. After all, you're my favorite little sweetheart."

I rarely had candy or other treats, especially my
favorite—chocolate—but when I did, my mother always
cautioned, "Take only one, Jeanie, and say 'thank you.'"

So it was with some wariness that I took one of the cherries, unwrapped the red cellophane, and popped it into
my mouth. The cordial liquid leaked out of the corners of
my lips as I bit into the cherry and grinned at Uncle
Chester. I grabbed another, unwrapped it, put it in my
mouth, and then snatched a handful, each nestled in its
red wrapper. Having nowhere else to put them, I thrust
the candies into the pocket of my pale-blue winter coat.

I looked up at Chester in his army uniform. It was

wartime and he was on leave, visiting our family before going into combat. I thought he was wonderful and imagined that he'd meet my daddy, who was already fighting over there.

"Thank you," I uttered, and ran outside with my chocolate-laden pocket before he could change his mind. I was four years old.

All afternoon I climbed the crabapple tree in our neighbor's yard, jumped rope, played hopscotch, rode my tricycle, and balanced on a limb dangling near the edge of Peachtree Creek. Not until I went home for dinner did I remember the cherries.

Smashed. The gooey melted chocolate and liquid filling had oozed out and around the cellophane, filling my pocket. I cried and screamed because I wanted more candy. My mother screamed a bit, too, because getting the chocolate mess out of that wool coat was most difficult and she was furious.

Furious at me for being so greedy. At Chester for letting me have so many candies. At the war for taking Daddy away and leaving her to care for me while holding down a full-time job. Despite the war, I was sheltered and, for the most part, unaware of it except at night when I kissed Daddy's picture after I'd said my prayers and jumped into bed.

The war ended and Daddy finally came home after spending three years in hospitals and enduring twenty-one operations. Uncle Chester married and settled in the West after the war, far from our Atlanta home, but our families kept in touch.

We shared news of my engagement, and the week before the wedding a package arrived from across the country. I opened it and found a photo of a small brown-haired girl and a tall, handsome soldier. A note wished me much happiness with a teasing reminder that I'd always been his "favorite little sweetheart."

He remembered me. I couldn't believe that Chester still had that picture after all those years. Memories of my childhood flooded my mind. Then I looked more closely at the package. At the bottom, under a fluff of tissue, sat a box of chocolate-covered cherries.

Jean Stewart

3

RELAXING RENDEZVOUS

Sharing Chocolate

If any man finds the minutes too slow, and
the atmosphere too heavy to withstand;
let him be given a good pint of
amber-flavored chocolate ...
and marvels will be performed.

Jean-Anthelme Brillat-Savarin

I learned to share when I was little, just like all obe-
dient preschoolers. Most things, anyway.

I was a junior in high school when I first realized I hadn't learned to share chocolate. A handsome
senior I'd admired from afar asked me to go to a movie. I
hadn't expected even a smile as we passed in the school
hallways, so my stomach did flip-flops for three days until
date time. Tingles shot up and down my spine when, during the movie, he slipped his arm across the back of my
chair. Afterward, we stopped for ice cream. Sitting across
from him in a red vinyl booth, I carefully smoothed the
napkin on my lap and asked him to choose for both of us
whatever he liked best. He ordered a chocolate sundae
with two spoons. As we waited, our knees touched occasionally under the table. My heart fluttered at every
nudge. Our eyes met, I looked away, our eyes met again as

we talked about the movie we'd just seen, mutual friends, music we both liked.

The chocolate sundae arrived, a giant scoop of vanilla ice cream dripping with chocolate, adorned with a mound of whipped cream and a bright maraschino cherry. I took a delicate first bite and watched my date take a larger one. I allowed myself a slightly bigger second bite. He followed suit. Then the world closed in on the glass sundae dish. The ice cream cool on my lips. The chocolate moist and rich on my tongue. The whipped cream smooth as silk as it slid down my throat. Minutes passed before I became aware of my date laughing. The world widened again to include his grinning face, the table between us, and the sundae dish all but licked clean.

My face must have burned red as I gathered the courage to ask if he'd had even one more bite. Apparently not. He never asked me out again.

Lesson learned, I made sure I didn't shovel chocolate on subsequent dates. But with friends I must have grown lax. Years after the sundae debacle, when I was married and teaching my young children to share, I was dining with a group of three women friends. We'd stuffed ourselves on wild salmon and agreed to share a single slice of fudge cake.

I took my first, dainty bite. Some chocolate cake is too dry to truly savor, but not this delectable dessert. A thin line of raspberry filling separated two thick layers of dark, moist, daringly rich cake. A bittersweet ganache dripped over the top and sides. The next thing I noticed was one of the women shaking a finger at me. It seems that she and the other two women had gotten only two bites apiece, so sharp was my focus, so fast my fork as I ate far more than my share. I bowed my head before her scolding, begging their apologies, not meaning to be a bad friend.

Later that evening I confessed my behavior to my husband. He wrinkled his forehead in confusion. "Didn't you know you always do that?" he asked. "That's why I don't like to share desserts with you."

I slumped down in an easy chair and stared at the hooked rug under the ottoman. No matter what my intentions, I seemed to be shamelessly selfish when faced with chocolate.

What could I do? I didn't want to resign myself to dining alone, nor could I possibly say good-bye to gooey sweets when out with friends. Yet I seemed unable to share chocolate. After careful thought, I came up with an idea. What I needed was a friend who was equally chocolate-challenged. Together we could search out the most sumptuous desserts in the city.

By the time we'd finished off a shared chocolate mousse after our first lunch together, Janet and I knew we'd found our chocolate twin. We automatically, effortlessly matched each other bite for bite. We discovered two more women who perfectly completed a dine-out quartet. We all liked the same books, theater, and art, and always found a hundred things to talk about. But incomprehensibly, they didn't care that much for chocolate.

Now, on a regular basis, we get together. We chat nonstop through hors d'oeuvres and entrees. Then it's time for dessert. One of the women usually has the strength of character to forego dessert in the interest of staying slim.

Another's tastes run to pumpkin cheesecake, a Swedish cream, or a fruity sorbet. Janet and I invariably order some chocolate thing to divide. The exact nature of the sweet varies. It might be a silken panna cotta, a bittersweet chocolate torte, a chocolate tiramisu, or simply a double fudge brownie. The way we eat it never varies. We start at opposite sides of a plate or dish with a fork or spoon, take our first bite, and never look up until our utensils have met in the middle. Possibly we don't even breathe between bites. We both know that if one of us pauses for even a fraction of a second, the other will, without a doubt, swoop in for an extra morsel of chocolate.

Some things just aren't possible to share.

Samantha Ducloux Waltz

A Chocolate Tradition

When life gets sticky, dip it in chocolate.

Cyndy Salzmann, Crime & Clutter

I n a world of uncertainty and chaos there is one thing we can count on: chocolate. It is always milk, dark, or white. Good chocolate will melt in your mouth and all over your hands. But for me, eating good chocolate brings back some of the sweetest memories of my childhood. Not many families are blessed to have a family tradition centered on chocolate, but I was raised in one that did.

Every year on the day after Thanksgiving while the men of the family were gathered around the television watching football, the women would converge on my grandparents' house and turn it into a chocolate dipping factory. No area of the house was safe from powdered sugar explosions or chocolate splatters. The kitchen became prep-central. It was a room of busy hands and bustling people. Here, the fondants and fudges were rolled; the caramels were cut; and the nuts were chopped, sorted, or mixed. Once this was done they were placed on trays and delivered to the dippers. The dippers were set up in the dining room. One end of the table was covered with a granite slab. At the top of the slab was a double boiler used to melt the chocolate chunks located in a large bowl to the right.

As I grew older, I was allowed to tend the chocolate and to this day I can recite in my sleep the lectures received on the proper way to melt, stir, and maintain chocolate. I think it was the year I turned fourteen that I was first allowed to try my hand at dipping. I was so excited that I scrubbed the top layer off my hands and arms when told to go wash up. I must not have done too badly because every year thereafter I was stationed at the dipping table. Once dipped, the chocolates were transferred to the cooling room. It was actually the master bedroom, and it was my favorite room to be in on dipping day. When you walked into the cooling room the sweet smell of cooling chocolate assaulted you. There was also the bonus that you were all alone, surrounded by a huge variety of freshly cooled chocolates, and no one cared if a few went missing.

After the dipping and cleanup of the prep area were done, we had a lunch of turkey sandwiches and leftover pie. Though exhausted from rolling, cutting, dipping, carrying, marking, melting, mixing, and cleaning, we still had two things left to do: put each and every chocolate into a paper candy cup and then we had to box it. With all six of us at the same task for the first time during the day, putting the chocolates into cups went fairly quickly. Then came boxing.

All year the adults had been squirreling away boxes and tins for this event. We each grabbed a box, and as we bumped into and tripped over one another, we worked our way around the room to obtain a tasty variety for each box. Usually we were so tired we boxed in near silence. The rustling of candy cups and boxes and tins opening and closing was like a song we each danced to. I always did my own box first. It was payment for my work throughout the day. I loved the lemons, oranges, and mints the best. My box was not meant to be full of variety; it was meant to be a reward—so I stocked it with only my heart's desire.

I don't ever remember an argument about who got more or someone feeling cheated. There was always enough. After boxing we would pile into our cars and head home, eager for a warm shower and excited to hand out boxes of our homemade, hand-dipped chocolates to long-time friends and neighbors. I am the oldest granddaughter, and the year I went to college I missed our chocolate tradition. It's been years, and we haven't all gotten together to dip since. Every fall, as the air dips to a perfect "cooling room" temperature, I think

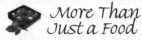

More Than Just a Food

Over the centuries many cultures have used the seeds of the cacao tree as a sacred symbol in religious ceremonies and for medicinal remedies.

The Mayans and Aztecs used cacao beans as currency and gave the beans as gifts at important celebrations.

In the 1600s, when Spanish royalty married, they gave cocoa as part of the dowry.

A prisoner serving three life terms in solitary confinement at Pelican Bay Penitentiary leaches the color from the coating of M&M's and uses it as ink in painting postcards that sell for $500 each. Proceeds are donated to a fund that supports children of prisoners.

about those days spent dipping. Memories of the taste of a fondant ball snatched off a tray on the way to the dining room, shouts for more chocolate chunks, my arm aching from hours of dipping, somehow finding chocolate on my forehead, being so tired that everything is funny, a feeling of kinship and peace, and the fun of being with just the girls melt over me.

My family has known about the benefits of chocolate for years. When I eat a good chocolate, though no chocolate has ever compared to the ones my family made, I inhale the intoxicating aroma, and as the chocolate takes over my senses, I relive the feeling of happiness that comes from being surrounded by family—and chocolate.

Christina Dymock

The Gift of Chocolate and Love

I'll eat anything, as long as it's chocolate.

Author Unknown

M y memories of my dad after his stroke are mostly of him sitting in a chair eating candy. He could no longer work, so my mom was left to support our family of five.

I wasn't a deprived child except when it came to my dad's nonpareils, those yummy round chocolates with white sugar beads on top. They were my dad's favorite, his one luxury, and he always had some. My mouth watered every time I saw them sitting next to him. Oh, how I wanted to take the whole bag and stuff them into my mouth.

I'd watch my dad eat those candies and beg with my eyes. Every now and then it worked and he gave me one. I was in heaven when I was given a nonpareil. I tried to make it last as long as possible by picking off the sugar beads and eating them one at time and finally letting the chocolate slowly dissolve in my mouth.

I never forgot how good those nonpareils were and vowed that someday I would have a whole bag of them.

My dad had another stroke and died when I was twelve.

Years later at a grocery store I saw a bag of nonpareils and bought them. As my little girl and I sat and ate them, I told her about my dad. The memories were bittersweet.

I lost my mom when I was twenty-one. Before she died, she gave me her first diamond ring from Dad. I gave it to my older sister so she could have the diamonds put in another setting. She said that someday when I was more settled she would give it back to me so I could pass it on to my daughter. I thought about it through the years. It was beautiful, full of memories, and I wanted it. I didn't want to seem greedy or take it from her so I never asked about it.

On my thirty-third birthday, my sister said she had a special gift for me, and I thought, *Good, the ring*. She handed me a beautifully wrapped box that was too big and too heavy to be the ring. I was a little sad. As I took the paper off the box I saw the words "Marie's Homemade Candies." Marie's is the best melt-in-your-mouth candy I have ever tasted. I didn't get it too often because it was very expensive and I couldn't afford it. I cried when I opened the box and there before my eyes were three pounds of Marie's "made especially for me" nonpareils.

Wow, what a gift! I popped one (okay, three) into my mouth. Everyone was joking about how I should be like Dad and not share them as they each took a couple. When the box was handed back to me I saw a glitter and shook the box. There, peeking out of all those nonpareils, was the ring.

For the first time in my life I was speechless, partly because I had a mouth full of that delicious candy and partly because I was overtaken by emotion. I was thrilled to get the ring, but the gift of nonpareils stirred my emotions like nothing else could have. Who would ever think that chocolate could mean so much? For me the gift of chocolate nonpareils was truly the gift of love.

Merrie Root

Chocolate—Eat Your Heart Out

Chocolate was bad for us, now they're saying it's healthy. That news didn't surprise me
any. I always knew Hershey's would look
great in an I.V. bag.

Martha Bolton

For years, I ate healthy foods simply because I had read they were good for me. As each new food was touted as the perfect one to turn back aging or stop a heart attack in its tracks, I added it to my grocery cart.

I ate broccoli, tofu, wheat germ, and oat bran—trying first one miracle food and then another, only to find I couldn't keep up with science. Half the time the research was faulty (the mice only pretended to eat the food and then ordered in pizza), or it was financed by the guys who produced the miracle food in the first place. If the research was okay, two weeks later something better came along, at least until it also got thrown out with yesterday's news.

Deep in my heart of hearts, I hoped that one day chocolate would be hailed as the newest health food. Well, my prayers have been answered. Chocolate, that luscious, sweet, melt-in-your-mouth ambrosia of the gods, is actually good for you.

It took a while to fumble my way through all the sciencespeak, but the bottom line is that chocolate makes the natural chemicals in our bodies produce a feel-better feeling—a natural high. It's the same high that runners get after a long race, but chocolate does all the work for you. You don't even have to leave the privacy of your house, sweat, or wear spandex.

Researchers have spent years and millions of dollars to discover this. Silly researchers. Like most women, I've known it intuitively. Many a chocolate has given its life for me when I've stumbled my way out of an unhappy relationship. It's also nourished my soul during rough patches at work, particularly long winters, or even broken nails.

Chocolate is versatile. It's also been with me as I celebrated new relationships, promotions at work, and finding a new lipstick in just the right shade to match my new sweater. In other words, chocolate is like a best friend and lover all rolled up into one very tasty package. While it can't hug you or take out the garbage, chocolate is smart enough to mimic the brain chemistry of romantic love and it's as close as the corner store.

Unlike some men, a box of chocolate won't leave you for a younger, thinner, or richer woman. And I've never heard of a chocolate that had a fear of intimacy or problems making a commitment. Chocolate is simply there for you. Move over broccoli, here comes chocolate. Aha, I can hear you saying: "A minute on the lips, a lifetime on the hips." Do you really want hips that are so sharp you can saw wood on them? No, you want rounded feminine hips. Hips that say "I am woman." At least that's what my hips say and they're very happy hips, thank you. Besides, while your hips may be getting a little rounder, your heart is getting stronger. Although chocolate contains saturated fat, it also contains high levels of antioxidant chemicals that lower your risk of heart disease. It's not only good for broken hearts in the romantic sense, but also it could prevent one, in the medical sense.

I can see it now. Millions of people turning their backs on tofu, bran, and broccoli and heading for the nearest candy store. Drugstores and health stores shelving chocolate bars next to the vitamin pills. Mothers begging their children to eat more chocolate. The Easter bunny becoming a national health symbol as doctors tell patients to take two chocolates and call them in the morning.

I don't know about you, but I'm going to put my feet up, get a glass of red wine in one hand and a chocolate in the other, and indulge to my heart's content. And if scientists need more subjects for clinical trials, I hereby volunteer my services. It's the least I can do for the advancement of medical science.

Harriet Cooper

Is There Chocolate in Heaven?

Carefully prepared chocolate is as healthful
a food as it is pleasant; it does not cause
harmful effects to feminine beauty, but is on
the contrary a remedy for them.

Jean-Anthelme Brillat-Savarin

I n the perpendicular universe known as the
Amazon, an electric-blue macaw feather slowly
wafts from the hundred-foot-high branches of a
eucalyptus tree, passing torquata hummingbirds, leaf-
cutter ants, and lizards as it flutters to the dark rain forest
floor. It lands soundlessly amid ocelots and emerald boas
that slink and creep past parasitic insects and carnivorous
plants in search of their next meal.

Thankfully, only the squirrel monkeys consider the pods
of the giant cacao tree a treat, leaving millions of yellow-
green beans for Godiva, Ghiradelli, and Lindt to pick,
roast, grind, and whip into mouthwatering meltables for
chocoholics worldwide. Dubbed "the food of the gods"
(and "the fruit of the devil"), cocoa has inspired lovers,
poets, moviemakers, songwriters, novelists . . . and me.

My first memory of the slippery-when-softened stuff
was the Easter before my fourth birthday when Nonna

hid Hershey's Kisses and Circus Peanuts in her cozy dining room. In no time, the cotton-candy-pink dress I'd worn to church bore streaky evidence of my finds, and my newfound addiction. From that day on, pennies found and dimes earned clinked into the sole of my red plastic cowboy-boot bank—my jingling-jangling, chocolate-purchasing power.

When my daughters became discoverers of hollow bunnies and solid duckies that peeped from behind books and knickknacks, we invested our time and energies in creating our own delicacies. Neighbors raved over chocolate-smothered pretzels, cream cheese eggs, butter mints, and caramels that, packed into tins and delivered by my pigtailed, giggling girls, marked the season. Soon birthday party invitations were almost always accompanied by "mommy requests": "Please bring some of your homemade, heart-shaped chocolate lollypops."

My husband started a family tradition by presenting our girls with their very own Big Red Heart of gooey chocolates on Valentine's Day, just like Mommy's. Year after year, they'd sit wide-eyed as he told them that Japanese beauties gave white chocolates to the men who'd captured their hearts, and how in some cultures, the cocoa bean—not the apple—is considered the first fruit.

Santa and reindeer chocolates, garbed in red and green tin foil, filled their Christmas stockings. Mugs of frothy cocoa, topped by bright white marshmallows, warmed fingers and toes turned icy cold by winter's biting wind. Cool chocolate milk washed down countless bologna sandwiches, and nothing said "welcome home" after a hard day of arithmetic and social studies like a pan of moist-and-chewy, fresh-from-the-oven chocolate brownies. And "chocolate" tacked on to the words pie, cake, pudding, or cookie painted smiles on even the most stubborn frownie faces.

Though our daughters are grown now, their dad still shops for heart-tugging cards to accompany chocolates he gives his "best girls" every February fourteenth. The delicacy marks their own anniversaries, and like their mom, they've learned gift givers can't go wrong . . . when inside the gaily wrapped package is a box of paper-skirted chocolates.

Whether experts judge it "rustic" or "snappy," chocolate—like few things in this world—has the power to sweeten the bitterest mood. Not even the most soothing symphony can stir the soul as a Hershey's bar can, and nothing but chocolate can turn pessimists into optimists who believe that if no one witnesses their consumption of Kisses or Melts, the calories don't count.

I can think of no better incentive to live by—The Golden Rule; war and sin and evil would cease, now and forever, if only we frail humans had proof . . . there's chocolate in heaven.

Loree Lough

Auntie Yum

Life is uncertain—eat dessert first!

Author Unknown

Who would travel two and a half hours by plane, brave three hours of Seattle traffic, then take a forty-five-minute ferry ride for a piece of bakery-bought cake on a cheap paper plate? Me. Aunt Syd. I wasn't about to miss my nephew's first taste of chocolate.

It was a typical firstborn's one-year-old party—adults sipping wine, snacking on appetizers, requesting "just a sliver" of cake, and discussing music, politics, weather, books, and work, accompanied by rock music from my brother's iPod. No one paid much attention to the children, not even the birthday boy.

Except me. I had waited out Peace Corps duty, a new house purchase, and years of career development for my brother to make me an aunt. My sister-in-law has three sisters, so I've tried my best to stand out: Aunt Syd's Book & Occasional Toy Club, phone calls, a handful of visits, and now I was there for the first birthday. The first piece of cake. The first taste of chocolate.

I sat straight across from Quinn's highchair, camera ready, and waited for him to explore his cake. Quinn gazed down at his plate and stuck one tentative finger into the dark frosting.

At first I had been dismayed that the cake was not homemade, but I had to give Holly B's credit. Her bakery makes a moist, decadently rich chocolate cake. Better than most birthday cakes, especially the ones from a boxed mix. I waited, snapping a quick "before" picture.

Quinn stuck one frosting-covered finger into his mouth. His forehead wrinkled in momentary confusion. Oh no, I fretted. He doesn't like it. Then his eyebrows shot up. And his hand plunged down into the cake.

"Yum. Yum," I said, snapping a picture. Quinn stuck two fudgy fingers into his mouth, while his other hand pinched off a chunk of chocolate cake. The next bite left a thin brown mustache on his lip, turning him into a wispy-haired Clark Gable.

After attending several first-birthday parties, I've come to believe that you can tell a lot about people from the way they approach their first piece of chocolate cake. My daughter Emma ate her miniature birthday cake by gently swiping one finger through the frosting and daintily placing it in her mouth. She never even needed a napkin. Her friend Anna, on the other hand, stood beside Emma's highchair grabbing fistfuls of cake and plunging them into her mouth. Eleven years later, Emma still approaches life with hesitant grace, while Anna surges into it with abandon.

Quinn devoured several chunks of cake with both hands, pausing every now and then to suck on a particularly tasty fist.

"Yum. Yum," I repeated as Quinn's chocolate mustache

grew into a goatee, then a beard. Bits of cake stuck in the collar of his shirt, and flecks of frosting speckled his plump little tummy.

A well-meaning party guest approached Quinn's chin with a paper towel. I blocked her hand, maybe a bit too aggressively.

"No, let him stay messy," I scolded, then snapped another picture. I refrained from reminding the woman that I was Quinn's aunt, even though I live 900 miles and a ferry ride away. And she had no business whatsoever to put herself between me and Quinn's first piece of chocolate-frosted nirvana. When she'd first arrived at the party, this same woman had taken Quinn into her arms with a familiarity I didn't have with my own nephew. I'd actually felt jealous, like a wife whose husband overtly flirts with other women. *You're mine,* I thought. My family. Not hers.

Another guest made a comment about Quinn always associating chocolate with flashing lights.

"You only have one first piece of chocolate cake," I replied, zooming in for a close-up of Quinn's thickly frosted face.

"Yum," I said to Quinn as he scraped the last sticky globs of frosting from his plate with the edge of his closed fist.

Quinn removed his fist from his mouth just long enough to reply. "Um."

"Yum," I repeated.

Quinn smiled. "Um," he answered.

He looked down at his empty paper plate, then lifted it with one hand and licked the center, marking the tip of his nose with frosting. Soon the back of the paper plate was coated in as much chocolate as the front. Quinn grabbed the plate with both sticky hands and sucked on its ruffled edge. His cheerful thoroughness impressed me. Will this be a character trait that persists? A few minutes later he managed to roll his plate into a tube that he held with both hands and jammed into his mouth. Removing it only to answer my "yums" with his "ums."

During the rest of my visit, Quinn frequently caught me with his big blue eyes and said "um."

"Yum," I answered every time, making him grin and wiggle with delight.

I get to see Quinn for only a few days every few months, and I probably won't ever share in his daily routines, but I hope we have forged a lasting chocolate bond. Maybe I'll have to start Aunt Syd's Book & Occasional Toy *and* Chocolate Club.

Auntie Yum, I thought as I sailed away on the ferry boat. Now that's something I hope lasts a long, long time.

Sydney Salter Husseman

A Fudgeless Fridge

Man cannot live by
chocolate alone—but woman can!

Author Unknown

I am in a desperate search for chocolate, and I know that somewhere in my refrigerator I have long ago hidden a secret supply. I am rustling past the veggie cheese slices, the veggie pepperoni, the veggie hot dogs, the veggie Canadian bacon, and the expired tofu (all my husband's) in search of my Mecca.

There is a lifetime-supply-size container of salsa that I bought impulsively at Sam's Club, which now takes up way too much space. There's an empty pitcher that once held orange juice, now waiting on deck for the dishwasher. I am moving past Gladware containers filled with watery mashed potatoes, leftover cheese pizza, and salad with brown lettuce. I know there must be fudge in my fridge somewhere.

The freezer. There is a red tray of heart-shaped ice cubes and three boxes of garden veggie burgers: savory mushroom, sautéed onion, and flame grilled. An open box of cheese and onion pierogies is spilling out in the icy back corner, but there is not a drop of chocolate around. I would lick it up if there were, even if it meant getting my tongue stuck to the icebox.

The freezer holds my dreams, half-finished, destined for the trash. There is a yogurt container full of homemade babaghanoush, an ambitious project one night, now long forgotten. Frozen gourmet apple turkey sausages that were supposed to be destined for a tasty dinner on the grill . . . last summer, that is.

I toss this and that into the trash as I continue my search, feeling the chill. Just a little chocolate, a bite, to tide me over, to bridge the afternoon to the evening, to make up for the micro-inequities of life and maybe some of the macro ones, too.

Of course, if I were a refrigerator, I would keep my treasures hidden in the vegetable bins. So I bend over and pull open the drawer that's off its tracks. Before me are about two dozen onions in peeling brown paper skins, flaking everywhere, some growing long green stems, plus a bag of expensive shallots, ingredients for a delicious vichyssoise soup, never made, long forgotten, the recipe missing.

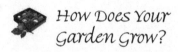

How Does Your Garden Grow?

Hershey's sells Cocoa Shell Mulch by the bag. The clean husk that is removed from the roasted cocoa bean is a by-product in the chocolate-making process. Too sweet to be true? Gardeners report that although it's more expensive than wood mulch, less is used, it deters insects, is weed-free, and is organic.

As an added bonus, it has a dark brown chocolate color, and, yes, it smells like chocolate! At least for the first few days.

One more bin to go, and inside is a plastic yogurt container full of forgotten homemade rum balls, a Christmas gift from a coworker, which I am allowing to marinate for several years.

Then a mirage, a vision from heaven. A Hershey's chocolate box, a wedding remnant that housed wedding favors: Hershey's chocolate bars with colorful, fancy, personalized labels with our names and our wedding date. I whip it open. There are about ten bars, and I squeeze one after the other in a frenzy. Each one squeezes into nothing but paper. A label and the foil, folded back up to look like a chocolate bar, saved for sentimental reasons. I have been here before.

Elizabeth Kann

House of Chocolate

All you need is love. But a little chocolate now and then doesn't hurt.

Author Unknown

T he majority of the time moms don't mind sharing. At the risk of sounding like a subnormal mom, however, I confess I don't like sharing my chocolate. I further confess to having hoarded chocolate. If there was only enough chocolate to give everyone one piece, that's the way it panned out, but if I was able to purchase an extra candy bar, I did. Only I didn't tell anyone. It was my little secret. Some days we mothers just need a little something to get us through. I figured if chocolate was what was keeping my sanity intact, so be it.

When our daughters, April and Lissie, were in elementary school and our young son, Nathan, was a rambunctious two-year-old, candy bar sales became a popular means of fund-raising at the school. Boxes and boxes of chocolate bars were sent home with both girls. For weeks we were selling chocolate bars. The scent of chocolate permeated our house. I was on a high that continued to rise with each passing day. But along with the responsibility of selling candy bars came the responsibility of not eating up the profits, and more important, making sure the children didn't end up with the same bad habit their mother had.

Our weekly bit of shared chocolate was quickly becoming a daily affair. I knew it could not continue. Being a mother came first, so the remaining candy bars were to be returned to the school. It was a sad day, to be sure. Our daughters, their eyes as wide as saucers, agreed, but their hearts were not in it. My husband said it was for the best. The only one who did not understand our sadness was our son. Nathan didn't even like chocolate.

The next day was cold and rainy. Rather than have the girls lug their boxes of candy bars to the bus stop in inclement weather, I decided to deliver the chocolate myself after their brother woke up. Pleased with my idea, April and Lissie raced to the bus stop. I checked on Nathan. Since he was still asleep, I took advantage of the time and headed to the laundry room. Almost immediately, I heard the large container of Legos crash to the floor in the living room. "Good morning, Nathan," I called.

"Morn-ing," his sing-song voice floated back to me. I smiled and peeked around the corner. He was sitting on the floor with his back to me, his blond curls in wild disarray on his bed-tousled head.

"Ready for breakfast?" I asked.

"Nope," he said as he began sorting blocks. "Making house. Making house," he sang.

"Okay. You make a house. Momma's going to finish this laundry. Okay?"

"Otay," he replied.

"Otay," I repeated, smiling as I returned to the laundry.

Every few minutes I called to Nathan, and he answered cheerfully. Surprised his attention span was holding out this long, but pleased he was playing contentedly, I folded two loads of tiny shirts and then tackled the laundry basket filled with towels and sheets. When I finished, I crawled on my hands and knees down the hall and hid behind the couch, hoping to surprise Nathan. He was so animated and engrossed in his play that he didn't notice me until I sprang out.

He squealed in delight then pointed to his masterpiece. "House!" he shouted excitedly. My mouth dropped open. My little boy had never built a more exquisite building. Bright yellow, red, and blue Lego blocks were stacked high on two sides. The other two sides were bricks of pure chocolate. Nathan beamed from ear to ear as my eyes followed the trail of candy wrappers across the living room floor.

After I praised Nathan for his delicious masterpiece, he helped me pick up the chocolate pieces and put them into a large Ziploc bag, which we then put in the freezer. Secretly we were all pleased. Nathan's chocolate house provided us with enough chocolate to indulge in once a week until the end of the school year. My husband be - lieves I subconsciously wanted the chocolate to remain in the house, so it was my thoughts that cajoled our son into becoming a chocolate architect that morning. I don't know and I don't care, I'm just grateful things turned out the way they did.

Helen Kay Polaski

Kisses for Daddy

Life without chocolate is life lacking
something important.

Marcia Colman Morton and Frederic Morton

M y daddy could have been the perfect Santa, with his chubby cheeks, wavy white locks, and jolly heart. And although he fit the bill, it's best he didn't play the part, because he'd eat all the candy canes.

For you see, like me, Daddy had a serious sweet tooth. And living in our house, you couldn't help but love sweets, because every evening Mom would serve up one of her scrumptious desserts like fudge brownies dripping with homemade chocolate icing. Ooh. I can almost taste the goodness.

Chocolate was like a fifth food group in our house. And to this day, it's still one of my favorite friends. Mom always packed a huge bag of goodies for our vacations from Michigan to Florida. And while traveling, I always knew when Daddy got a little bored or sleepy behind the wheel, because you could hear him crackling the Tootsie Roll wrappers as he tore into our sweet stash.

Daddy is and always will be my hero. And without a doubt, the most difficult day of my life was when Mom and I had to place him in a nursing home. Alzheimer's disease had slowly stolen the man we once knew, and now with his specialized needs, Mom could no longer care for him at home.

Daddy lived in a nursing home for several years, and every day Mom visited him at lunchtime to feed him. And because she knew how much he loved chocolate, she'd faithfully give him Hershey's Kisses at the end of each meal. Whenever I'd take a turn to feed Daddy, before leaving home I could always count on a call from Mom asking, "Honey, could you stop by my house to pick up your Dad's candy on the way?"

"Sure, Mom," I reluctantly answered one day, thinking it seemed silly stopping the car just to pick up a few pieces of chocolate. What difference will it make anyway? Dad doesn't even know who we are. But I honored Mom's wishes and picked up the candy, tucked it in my purse, and hurried on my way to see Daddy.

While spoon-feeding Daddy his pureed food that day, the song "Butterfly Kisses" began playing over the dining room radio. And as I sat listening to those beautiful words penned by a loving father for his daughter's wedding day, I could hardly stand the pain of looking into the blank stare of my father's eyes.

Daddy, I wish you could remember me, I thought, while wiping away tears. Oh, what I'd give for you to have one lucid moment where the two of us could just talk about life.

But he kept staring at me as if wondering, "Who are you?"

Feeling overwhelmed with grief, I thought, *I'm just*

*going to wash Dad's face, then wheel him back to his room for
his afternoon nap, and be on my way.*

But as I began cleaning Daddy's face, he glanced up at
me with the most inquisitive look, and I heard him faintly
whisper, "Candy?"

"Oh, Daddy!" I exclaimed while wrapping my arms
around him and hugging tightly. "I almost forgot your
Kisses!"

So, I quickly grabbed the bag of Hershey's Kisses out of
my purse, and as I gently pressed the first one through his
lips, I realized my sorrow had been replaced by the satis-
faction of being able to lavish love on Daddy with something he still enjoyed. Chocolate.

Daddy is in heaven now, but there's one thing I know
for sure. While chocolate can make us feel good for a
moment, a sweet heart will be remembered for a lifetime.

Peggy Morris

Sharing Sinful Indulgences

One of life's mysteries is how a two-pound
box of chocolates can make a woman
gain five pounds.

Author Unknown

After two months of dieting, this was the night of
the Big Treat. My husband, Sam, and I were sup-
porting each other in our quest for better health
and better bodies. Both of us were attempting to stay
within the guidelines of our diets, both of us were exercis-
ing, and both of us were measuring losses in weight and
inches.

All of that changed when I discovered chocolate diet
bars.

I had been at the grocery store earlier in the day and did
my usual stalking for new indulgences. On a regular basis
I would search the aisles at the grocery store for products
that were good for dieters.

On one such trip, I discovered ready-to-drink diet milkshakes. These drinks were like a sign from above that dieting was not going to be so bad after all. I chose chocolate
fudge for myself and strawberry for Sam. These drinks
became a very filling and satisfying staple.

On this day, I found the four-packs on sale. I filled my cart.

Then, right next to the diet milkshakes, I discovered diet nutrition bars. I had seen them before and others like them, but I ignored them. With this diet, I was mentally trying to change my approach to food and eating. If I started buying what looked like candy bars, I was just substituting one bad habit for another, I thought.

Regardless, I could not help noticing these tasty-looking chocolate treats. How could these hurt?

But then there was a clincher. The nutrition bars were on sale. Normally these bars were about two dollars apiece. Today they were half price with no limit to how many I could buy. Someone was out there looking after me, giving me the thumbs-up on this product. It was a sign.

So I bought a few.

Well, okay, a few is understating what I bought, but there were so many tasty choices from which to choose: Chocolate Cookies and Cream, Chocolate Chip Brownie, Chocolate Cream Pie, Chocolate Almond Brownies, Mocha Chocolate Decadence, and Chocolate Toffee. I was out of control in diet chocolate heaven.

While loading up my cart, I noticed one more choice: Chocolate Caramel. Chocolate caramel was Sam's all-time favorite. Sam talked in his sleep, saying, "Chocolate caramel. Chocolate caramel. Chocolate caramel." I heard him describe furniture with sentences like, "The chair was an interesting shade of chocolate caramel."

That brought me back to reality.

I unloaded what I had put in my cart and kept only two

of each type in my basket. My thoughts were simple. What harm would it be if Sam and I shared these bars after dinner? The damage would be halved.

When Sam got home from work, I had the bars laid out for him on the kitchen counter. His first reaction was, "I thought we weren't going to do these." Then he saw the chocolate caramel bar. "Chocolate caramel?" he said as if hypnotized. "You know, I love chocolate caramel. These bars have to be healthy."

Enough said. The bars got Sam's seal of approval.

After dinner, we prepared our coffee. Then Sam got out his ruler and divided the chocolate caramel bars in half. He didn't even ask what my preference was. Then carefully, with his sharpest knife, he cut the first bar in half. Each half went on a dessert plate we use for company. Each plate got a fork and a knife. "Small bites will make it last longer," Sam said. Each half was about an inch and a half long.

While relaxing in front of the TV, we both indulged in our first treat in months. It did not taste bad, but it was not my homemade chocolate cake that we had both pigged out on over the years. We took little bites as we sipped our coffee. We compared notes and opinions on this new discovery. If you ask Sam, he will tell you that I was making the same sounds I make when he massages my back. It wasn't my homemade chocolate cake, but it *was* chocolate!

"Another one?" my husband asked as he finished.

"Nope," I said. "That would be cheating. That would be going back to our old ways."

"But your piece was bigger," Sam sulked.

I pushed my last tiny knife-cut morsel toward Sam. "Here," I said, "this should make it even."

Sam looked at me as I nodded my head. Then he swallowed the last crumb and patted his newly flat belly.

Felice Prager

"I can gain weight just using suntan oil with cocoa butter!"

Reprinted by permission of Stephanie Piro. ©2002 Stephanie Piro.

The Secret Ingredient

A nice box of chocolates provides your total
daily intake of calories in one place.

Author Unknown

Mama was known far and wide for her fabulous fudge. She made it every year at Christmas and shared it with only family and dear friends—very dear friends. "It's too good to give it to just anybody," she always said, with a twinkle in her eyes.

The fudge was rich and chocolaty, smooth and creamy, and full of pecans—the best fudge in the world, we all agreed. There was some ingredient in it we couldn't quite identify. But when we asked, Mama would simply laugh and tell us it was love.

Of course, we imagined the unidentified ingredient had to be something exotic, but discovering Mama's secret was like trying to catch Santa Claus coming down the chimney. I remember watching her stir up a batch and trying to catch her adding that mysterious element, but she was far too clever for me. "Why don't you chop the pecans?" she'd suggest, handing me a knife and chopping board and directing me to the kitchen table. By the time my chore was done, she had already added whatever it was that made her fudge so special.

"Where'd you get the recipe, Mama?" I asked, handing her the bowl of chopped nuts.

"Your grandmother gave it to me when I married your father. Maybe I'll give it to you when you marry."

I grew up and married, but Mama wouldn't share the recipe. I asked for it one Christmas, but she smiled and patted my shoulder. "I'll give it to you when the time is right. I'm not ready to part with it just yet. After all, a woman has to have a few little secrets to make life interesting!"

For years I asked Mama for the recipe, and every year she would wink and tell me it wasn't yet time to share her culinary secret. It became a game we played that made us all laugh, but Mama would not give up that recipe! So I learned to make divinity, and even tried my hand at making fudge. But it never tasted like Mama's.

When Mama died suddenly one summer, my grief was overwhelming. I would catch myself reaching for the telephone to call her for advice, only to realize she wasn't there anymore. Then Christmas came, and I thought my heart would break. I made peanut brittle that year. It was delicious, but it wasn't Mama's special fudge.

By spring I was beginning to feel the raw edges of grief subside and decided to take on the task of organizing Mama's belongings. I had packed them hastily when her house sold. The first box I opened was filled with books, and I lost myself in happy childhood memories of stories she had read to me: *The Call of the Wild, Little Women, Aesop's Fables*. Then I discovered a book I didn't recognize, an old cookbook from a church Mama attended before she and Daddy married.

I cracked it open to a recipe for corn bread dressing. Mama had penciled notes in the margin: "Add one tbs. sage and an extra egg." I touched her neat handwriting and felt somehow close to her.

"I miss you, Mama," I said out loud, and then laughed at myself for being so maudlin.

Leafing through the cookbook, I found other recipes she had marked. Next to Chicken à la Panna, she had written, "Served to Garden Club 5/89—everyone raved." Melinda's Mandarin Orange Salad had a big star by it. "Jim's favorite!" her note said. She had always served it on Daddy's birthday. She had written "Ruthie's engagement party" next to Pork Tenderloin with Cranberries. I remembered that special night and smiled at the memories.

Then a loose piece of paper fell out of the book. I unfolded it, and my heart nearly stopped. It was a recipe in Mama's handwriting for Mother's Love Fudge, dated 1951. In a flash, I knew this was it—Mama's famous fudge recipe that my grandmother had given her long ago. Tears sprang into my eyes, and I laughed out loud again, feeling a bond with both Mama and my grandmother. I checked the ingredients and shook my head in wonder. I had them all, and Mama was right. The secret was in the love.

Ruth Jones

The Dud in White

Chocolate is cheaper than therapy
and you don't need an appointment.

Anonymous

I have a love-hate relationship with chocolate. You're probably thinking, "Yeah, yeah, most women do," but I promise you, my love-hate relationship is different. It has nothing to do with weight or health or escapism.

It all began some forty years ago. Friends and I were going to the Arlene Theater to see *Bye Bye Birdie*. The day promised to be super special because we had permission from our parents to walk all over town when the movie was over. At fourteen, this was a major achievement. We could linger in Woolworth's and get a cherry lemonade at the counter. We could ride up and down the escalator in the Fedway store as many times as we wanted. We could walk from one end of town to the other and back again, and we could flirt with boys. I went to bed fantasizing about this new freedom I'd never tasted before.

The first kink in my plans was when my mother told me what I had to wear.

"I don't want to wear that."

She laid the white sack dress across my bed. "You're going to."

"Why?"

"Because I said so."

"I hate that dress."

"You'll wear it or you won't go."

Stupid white sack. I hated it from the moment it was given to me. Some dumb hand-me-down from a cousin who was probably thankful to get rid of it. Bet Ann-Margret never wore anything she didn't like.

The theater was dark. My friends and I bought popcorn, a cola, and some Milk Duds before the show started. We snuggled into the center section, and I don't mind telling you I wiggled in my seat when Conrad Birdie made his first appearance. I wondered if I would resemble Ann-Margret if I wore my hair down. Trouble was my mom would never let me wear my hair down. It was ponytail or pigtails for me.

And stupid white sack dresses.

When the movie ended, we giggled our way into the sunlight, prissing like Ann-Margret and wondering aloud if we'd ever have our very own Bobby Rydell or Conrad Birdie. We danced down Methvin Street, singing "We love you, Conrad, oh, yes, we do—ooo." Could we draw any more attention to ourselves if we tried? I think not. The five of us laughed and sang to our hearts' delight, knowing our parents would probably find out because everyone knew everyone else, and someone always told.

Being the shy one of the group, I had an Ann-Margret moment and let down my long blonde hair. I twisted and twirled all around town, and up and down the Fedway store elevator. I was out of control. I even flirted with the boy at the Texaco Station on the corner of Main and Cotton streets. I never wanted the day to end.

We girls danced and raced one another back to the theater where our parents were to pick us up. And that's where my world came crashing down.

"What's that on the back of your dress?"

"What? Nothing. Where?" *Stupid white sack,* I thought.

"Ewwwww, you had an accident!" my friend pointed.

"I did not. What is it?"

"Poop!"

"No, it's not!" I could feel my face grow hot and knew it flamed red.

I pulled at the back of the ugly white dress and twisted to investigate. Something brown and gross-looking smeared across my rear.

Chocolate?

Milk Duds? I felt like a dud.

My life flashed before my eyes, and I remembered how I'd danced and shrieked around town, pretending to be Ann-Margret. I felt betrayed by the ugly white sack dress and the mom who made me wear it.

To this day, I can't eat chocolate without remembering and feeling embarrassed. And to this day, I never wear white.

Never!

Jessica R. Ferguson

It Turns to Love

There's more to life than chocolate,
but not right now.

Author Unknown

M y stepdaughter, Laura, gave me dirty look number three and stomped up the stairs, mumbling something, after being told to redo her homework.

I repeated my instructions at the back of a tie-dyed shirt as it disappeared around the corner. Reeling in frustration, I grabbed a cup of hot water and a spoon, and tore open a packet of silky brown powder for some hot chocolate therapy.

The heavenly aroma transported me to another evening, another place—five years ago, when Laura was nine. On the first night of our first-ever cruise, after a day of travel and a decadent four-course meal, my husband and I were exhausted.

By 11 PM we both lay in bed, him snoring and me struggling to keep my eyes open long enough to coordinate the next day's family activity schedule.

Laura would probably enjoy the scavenger hunt, I thought. I could drag Dan to a line-dancing class.

As I nodded off, I jolted to a tap on my shoulder. "Here,

take your glasses off when you sleep."

As her father does every night at home, a freshly scrubbed Laura, her own glasses steamy from the hot bathroom, kindly removed mine, and placed the activities schedule on the bedside table before it would have dropped to the floor. And as always happens at home, the movement and the talk woke me completely.

Laura looked adorable in her puppy-dog pajamas and smelled of floral soap and toothpaste. But I knew that sweet looks and smells and kind deeds could be deceiving. Even a stepmom could easily deduce that the thought of a weeklong separation from her regular life, especially from her mom, was particularly troublesome to Laura.

The photo of my husband, myself, and her—pained expression included—taken upon entering the ship, would be a lasting testament to the child's lack of excitement over going away with us.

I think I glared at Laura then and she just looked at me. *Okay, which one of us is being the child here?* I thought.

Suddenly I remembered something that I hoped she would enjoy, even if she was a grouchy little traveler. I held a quiet hope that maybe our one common interest, besides her daddy of course, could help us connect.

"Wait, hon, let me see, there's something in that brochure about a midnight party." I handed Laura a glossy photo of a table loaded with assorted chocolate goodies and the accompanying announcement.

Wide-eyed excitement brightened her face then, and she was full of questions: "Is this for real? Is it free? Can we go? Do we really wear our pajamas?"

"Well, it says right here, 'Midnight Madness Chocolate Lover's Pajama Party, All-You-Can-Eat Chocolate Buffet, Sunday night in the Grand Room,' so, yeah, let's do it."

A few moments later I freshened my face and brushed my hair, then jotted a quick note to my husband: "Gone to the chocoholic bash! *Yum.*"

"Look, an awesome chocolate fountain . . . and the fudge . . . double-dipped strawberries . . . this is sooo cool!" That's what Laura said before we high-fived and then shamelessly dove into the smorgasbord of cocoa confections set before us.

Neither of us minded that we were the only ones who had taken the words *Midnight Madness Pajama Party* literally. Our white robes and fuzzy slippers must have seemed a bit out-of-place amidst a sea of sequined dresses, tuxedos, and snooty looks; but we didn't care. We were a couple of giddy chocoholics out late and living it up.

The next morning, lying in bed, I whispered the details of our date to my husband, how we had giggled when we shared a secret and how we had been slightly embarrassed at being the only ones in our pj's, yet it had been the highlight of the night.

I smiled each time I mentioned how many times Laura had thanked me and how I'd had so much fun with her.

Now that Laura is fourteen and the little girl years are gone, our relationship seems to grow more complicated. Sometimes I'd like to rewind to a simpler time. I'd like to wear fuzzy ducky slippers and relive that magical chocolate party night, when we were two fancy-free girls on a lark.

Maybe she could also use some chocolate therapy, chocolate friendship. *Does chocolate shared turn to love?* I wondered. It's time I yelled up those stairs again,—"Laura, let's make brownies!"

Rhonda C. Leveret

Thank You, Santa

Any sane person loves chocolate.

Bob Greene

E very Christmas Eve, for as far back as I can remember, Santa Claus left M&M's in my stocking.
He wasn't lazy about it, either. The jolly old fellow didn't just pull store-bought bags from his pack and
drop them into the quilted plaid stocking nailed to the
mantle in my family's living room. He took his time with
the project, separating the festive red and green candies
from the others. Those were the days before the factory
packaged them in special color combinations for the holidays. Santa even twisted them into neat little cellophane
bundles tied with curly ribbons.

When I turned six, Santa began delighting me with both
plain and peanut versions of my favorite chocolate candy.
He left other goodies in my stocking, too. Crayons and
hair barrettes and fuzzy winter mittens when I was
young, nail polish and lip gloss and juicy tangerines as I
grew older. But the M&M's were always what I looked forward to most.

It just wouldn't have been Christmas without them.

Time passed. I grew up, married, and moved far away

from my parents and the home where I'd been reared. Most years I was able to visit sometime during the Christmas season. But when I couldn't, it was a sure bet that a package would arrive in my mailbox right before Christmas. Inside it would be my quilted plaid stocking. Inside the stocking I would find neat little packages of red and green M&M's bundled in cellophane and tied with curly ribbon.

It just wouldn't have been Christmas without them.

I was twenty-seven years old when my parents were killed in a tragic accident the day after Thanksgiving. I was devastated. As Christmas drew near, I grew more and more despondent. How could I face the holidays without my mom and dad? I cried myself to sleep on Christmas Eve. All I wanted to do on Christmas morning was pull the covers over my head and spend the day in bed feeling sorry for myself. But my husband would have none of that.

"Get up," he said, standing beside the bed with a steaming mug of coffee. "Have a couple of swallows of this and then let's go see what Santa brought." Taking my hand, he led me to the living room. There, nailed to the mantle over our little fireplace, was my quilted plaid stocking. Tears welled up in my eyes.

"Dump it out and let's see what you got," he said. I turned the stocking upside down and shook it. Out fell a box of crayons. Two bottles of nail polish. Some plastic hair barrettes. A tube of lip gloss. A pair of fuzzy winter mittens. Three juicy tangerines.

And finally, some neat little cellophane bundles tied

with curly ribbon, stuffed full with red and green M&M's, just like I'd received every Christmas from as far back as I could remember.

"Thank you, Santa," I whispered. "It just wouldn't be Christmas without these."

From somewhere high above, I knew Mom and Dad were smiling.

Jennie Ivey

The Old Red Devil

There are no Chocoholics Anonymous because nobody wants to quit.

Author Unknown

O n a Minnesota farm, there is no such thing as a meal without dessert. Early mornings, hard work, uncertainty, and a dread fear of the weather in all its extremes were the trade-offs for a life of Grandma's delicious, hearty meals capped with a little something sweet at the end, no matter what.

I grew up knowing that the cookie jar would always be full. There would always be a pail of ice cream the size of a rain barrel in the freezer. The middle drawer in Grandma's kitchen held a treasure trove of puddings and chocolate chips. Tiny jewel bottles of every sweet flavoring known to man twirled on the lazy Susan in the cupboard.

All of the best things started with butter and a big wooden spoon. Grandma and Grandpa had a dairy farm, and nothing but real sweet butter was ever acceptable in Grandpa's eyes. Once Grandma suggested a switch to margarine, but Grandpa, with an aghast, betrayed look, pointed toward the barn. "But, Marie! We raise cows!"

Grandma replied by pointing out her kitchen window

to the green fields that surrounded them. "Bill, we raise soybeans, too!"

Grandma had a huge mixing bowl, shiny as a new penny and big enough to use as a sled . . . not that any of us grandkids would know from experience. Sticks of butter unwrapped and softening in that bowl were like a sign from heaven. Something good was on its way.

Sometimes it was chocolate chip cookies that were the perfect middle ground between chewy and crispy. My mother mourned her inability to match those cookies every time she bit into one. Sometimes it was oatmeal cookies with plump raisins waiting to burst like rain clouds in your mouth. Or coffee cake with a crumbly layer of brown sugar and the ever-present mug of coffee every grown-up seemed to have. I had mine with a cold, jelly glass of milk flavored with a drop of Watkins vanilla.

But best of all, and more often than not, came the Old Red Devil. Grandma's cake was nine by thirteen inches of joy. Her version of devil's food was born from necessity, like so many things that come about in a farm kitchen. Just because milk soured was no reason to throw it away. Boiling water saved time by melting the butter, but it also stretched the milk. Cocoa powder instead of melted chocolate was more efficient and economical.

The incredibly flavorful white frosting was the result of a carton of New York vanilla ice cream accidentally melting on the countertop. It took the place of milk and butter, stirred together with a little powdered sugar into the easiest and most delicious icing I've tasted in my whole life.

But when all of those necessities collided in Grandma's

aluminum cake pan, her name written on all sides in black Magic Marker, something special was born. The cake was moist and substantial, but light enough for eager eaters to allow themselves to be convinced to have just one more small piece.

The "red" has always been a mystery. No food coloring is added, but the name makes you think you see a hint of scarlet all the same. The first time I saw Red Velvet Cake on a restaurant menu, I was blissful, thinking I had found Grandma's cake. I was wrong. It had none of the rich chocolate, none of the implied "fudginess" that a slice of Grandma's cake so sweetly offered and honestly delivered. The tang of the cream cheese frosting was nice, but there wasn't the smooth richness of Grandma's icing and the naughty knowledge that you really were having your cake and ice cream, too.

Chocolate cakes have come and gone for me. I've enjoyed them to their fullest, every slice, every bite, every last crumb pinched off the plate so it didn't get wasted. Brooklyn blackout cakes, flourless truffle tortes, mousse cakes with five kinds of chocolate, cheesecakes with ganache, and pound cakes studded with chunks of fudge: they've been devoured with relish. (Actually, with whipped cream and ice cream and Hershey's syrup and cherries.) I've made them myself. I've eaten them in some of the best bakeries and restaurants in the country. I've even used Grandma's recipe, in her own handwriting, stained with generations of batter and dusty with decades of cocoa and flour. But in all my life, in all the world, there will never be a cake like the Old Red Devil my grandma stirred up in the kitchen on the farm. And if you never got to sit at my grandma's table, well, you just don't have any idea what you've missed.

Lori Falce

 ### Try a Little Twist on Tradition

Barcelona, Spain, is home to some of the most innovative, exclusive chocolatiers in the world. One renowned shop, Enric Rovira, offers these unusual ingredients for their panned creations featuring 70-percent chocolate:

- salted pumpkin seeds, dark chocolate, dusted with licorice powder
- toasted, salted corn kernels, dark chocolate, dusted with cocoa powder
- deep-fried, salted pork skins, dark chocolate, dusted with cocoa powder
- toasted cocoa beans, white chocolate, dusted with powdered sugar
- roasted cacao nibs in dark chocolate
- single-origin Costa Rican and Kenyan coffee beans, dark chocolate, dusted with cocoa powder or powdered sugar.

The Game Plan

My therapist told me the way to achieve
true inner peace is to finish what I start. So
far today, I have finished two bags of M&M's
and a chocolate cake. I feel better already.

Dave Barry

M y son Patrick rushed in the door, letting it slam behind him.

"Mom, Mom, I get to go to Disneyland!"

"What, when? What are you talking about?" I asked.

"It's really easy! I only have to sell fifty boxes of chocolate candy bars and I can go. The coach said so."

"Whoa, slow down, kiddo. Do you know how many candy bars are in a box?"

"Nope, but everybody loves chocolate. I'll just sell them to all our friends."

I did the math on fifty boxes of chocolate bars and knew this was going to be quite a feat. But I hated to burst my six-year-old son's bubble.

"Patrick, we don't have that many friends to sell fifty boxes of chocolate to."

The look of disappointment on his face melted my heart. I certainly didn't want him going door-to-door, and my husband's office had a "no solicitation" policy.

Then I had a plan.

"Patrick, we'll do our best. Just wait until the end of the week."

Friday night rolled around and I dressed Patrick in his Little League uniform. It didn't hurt that he was very short and slim for his age and looked four years old.

We piled the boxes of chocolates into my VW bug and headed for the local mall.

I set up a card table in front of the bank. On top of it I placed just a single box of candy bars along with his baseball and mitt. We were playing it to the hilt. I gave him some last minute instructions.

"Wait until the person comes out of the bank. They'll have cash on them by then. Keep your candy bars out one box at a time. I'll keep the rest in the car. Tell people you only have one box left to sell and you're done."

Oh, God, I thought, *I'm going to hell for lying. Forgive me.*

"If you're not sure about a person, look at me and rub the brim of your baseball cap. I'll be parked over in the end stall. If I give you a thumbs-up, it's okay to approach them. Thumbs-down, stay away. You got it?"

He nodded, and we set our plan into motion. I settled down with a good book and a cola.

Patrick was a natural. He picked up the ball and tossed it from hand to hand between customers. He was so small and businesslike in his grey and blue uniform, people loved him.

Before long he was madly rubbing his cap.

I gave him a thumbs-up.

Pretty soon it was another rub of the brim. I gave him a thumbs-up again. Now I knew how coaches felt giving those strange signals from the dugout.

The candy bars flew through his hands. He didn't sell enough for his trip to Disneyland, but he did sell more than anyone else on his team. We ended up with some extra boxes, and I think we ate chocolate for a month after that. Our dentist seemed especially happy at our next visit.

Patrick is grown and still plays in a softball league. His wife warms the bench, cheering him on every Friday night. He called me last week.

"Hey, Mom, you wanna come watch me play some Friday?"

"This doesn't have anything to do with chocolate bars does it? Last time I got involved with you and baseball I remember selling a lot of chocolate."

He laughed. "No, Mom, the only chocolate you're going to see is the big chocolate bar I'm going to buy you from the snack shack."

"You're on," I replied.

Sallie A. Rodman

Heavenly Cookies

Life is like a box of chocolates. You never
know what you're gonna get.

Tom Hanks as Forrest Gump

When I was a child, chocolate called at me louder than Mom could yell. My first memory of tasting that delightful confection was when we lived in a small house behind my grandparents' home. Come to think of it, Grandma kick-started my chocolate yearning. As toddlers, my little brother and I watched *Howdy Doody* on television at Grandma's house. When we got on her nerves, she shooed us out to the yard.

One day my brother had tired of Clarabelle the clown and had already wandered up the walk to our house. I fidgeted around on Grandma's couch until I got on her nerves. "You must have ants in the pants! Here, take these cookies home and share them with your brother." She stuffed my little hands with four rectangular devil's-food cookies covered in a hard shell icing. Oh my, one bite of that tasty morsel and I was a goner. I shoved the second cookie into my mouth before I had devoured the first and would have died happily of chocolate asphyxiation if Grandma hadn't said, "Now, you save those other two for your brother."

Just then my mother leaned out our screen door and yelled, "Grandma, send her home. It's nap time." I had to think fast. I knew if I walked in the door with those cookies, they'd be gone. So I stacked the two remaining cookies on a tree stump, which was slightly taller than I was. I figured if I couldn't see them, no one else would find them. As soon as I awoke I would retrieve them. I ran up the walk, grinning and anxious to take my nap for a change. Mom offered me a sip of water but I shook my head no. I wanted to keep that delightful chocolate taste in my mouth as long as possible. I drifted off to sleep dreaming of my hidden treasure and pleasure.

When I awoke, I told Mom that I wanted to go to Grandma's. She unlatched the screen door and I darted. I planned my strategy as my little legs ran down the walkway: I would chomp down the hidden cookies, then I'd sit absolutely still on Grandma's couch. She wouldn't say that I had ants in the pants, and later I'd ask for another cookie.

When I reached the tree stump on that warm summer day, I stretched up on tip toe and felt around for my cookies—dismayed and alarmed at first when I couldn't find them, then elated when my fingers clasped the stack. I chomped into a cookie and chewed with ecstatic pleasure. My senses were alive.

I felt the tingle before I saw the trail of frenzied ants as black as the cookie I held in my hand scamper up my forearm. I screamed, I cried, I spat, I attracted all sorts of attention from Mom, Grandma, and the neighbors.

Grandma grabbed the garden hose and sprayed the

ants off my arm and out of my mouth. Nothing could calm me. I resisted Mom's hug, and ignored Grandma's request to calm down and take a deep breath. She scooped me up and told my mom she'd let me watch television.

I cried hysterically. Kicked and pleaded. "No-No-*No!*" There was no way I could ever go back into Grandma's house. She sat me down on the couch, and I jumped up and shook out my pant legs. "What are you doing, honey?" she asked.

I burst into tears again. "Getting the ants out of my pants," I cried.

"Oh, sweetheart, here, I got all of the ants off you; have a fresh devil's-food cookie and a glass of milk."

With the exception of devil's-food cookies, to this day I never refuse chocolate, especially now that the health-care professionals are spouting the benefits of flavonoids. Some days I feel like I'm five again and almost choke myself on dark chocolate.

Linda O'Connell

The Way Home

Coffee, chocolate, men . . . some things are
just better when they're rich.

Anonymous

G rowing up, one thing that made absolutely no
sense to me was why everyone made such a fuss
about chocolate. I couldn't stand chocolate cake.
Brownies were just all right, and chocolate ice cream never
rested inside my antichocolate stomach. I didn't even
share in our family tradition of hot cocoa. When the cool
months began to creep in and frost would blanket the
grass, my mom would break out the hot cocoa. Mom, my
sister, and my brother would all sit around savoring its
warmth. Me—I wouldn't even try it.

Seasons, holidays, and traditions came and went and I
found myself grown-up and enrolled in college a state
away from everything familiar. Gone were the voices of
my parents yelling through my bedroom door each morning for me to get up. Those voices were traded in for the
loud ring of my alarm clock thrusting me from dreamland
back to reality.

Out of everything that this new life brought me, my
loneliest times were coming back to a dorm filled with

strangers. No longer did the place where I laid my head each night bring a sense of security and comfort. Instead, when I looked around, I saw the unfamiliar.

Late that fall, as it began to turn cold, the stress of college life took its toll, and I just wanted to get away. I entered the one place that I thought I could find some solitude—my dorm room. Upon entering I discovered my roommate had all of her long-lost friends in our already jail-cell-size room. Frustrated, I turned around, wishing so badly that I could once again just walk into my brick country home in Missouri and see my family laughing as they drank from mugs of hot chocolate. The tradition that I once wanted no part of, I now longed to be in the midst of for the first time in my life.

Defeated, I walked with shoulders slumped to the campus mailroom and bookstore. I unlocked my mailbox, silently praying for just a word from home. Excitement swept over me as I reached my hand into the metal box, pulling out not one but two letters from home, one from my mother and one from my sister.

I walked down the flight of stairs and made my way to the exit. My hand was reaching for the doorknob when a familiar scent tickled my nose. A crooked smile split across my face as I turned back around and headed toward the back of the store. I reached for a cup, lined it up with the machine's long spout, and pushed the red button. Out came a gust of hot chocolate.

After filling the cup, I put a lid over the steamy liquid, paid for it, and headed out the door to the nearest vacant picnic table. Pulling out the letters from my pocket, I sat on the cool wooden bench and placed my cup of hot chocolate in front of me. I opened up my letters and began reading as I took a sip of the hot chocolate drink. Feelings of comfort and warmth flooded through my body. For the first time since I stepped foot on campus, I felt the peace that only home could bring me. The worries of my classes were gone, and the frustration with my roommate was forgotten. For the first time in my life, I joined in a tradition that I had snubbed my nose at so many times. As I warmed my hands on the heated cup, I laughed at the stories from my sister and smiled at words of love from my mother. Though miles had separated us, a cup of hot cocoa and a letter had brought us together that day.

I had heard chocolate referred to as comfort food many times in my life. On that day, sitting alone, miles away from home, chocolate became my link to a place that meant even more than just comfort. My hot-chocolate drinking tradition became my way back home.

Angela Gray

Chocolate's Belgian Roots

In 1857, Jean Neuhaus, a chemist in Brussels, began making chocolate tablets for medicinal reasons, but the popularity of chocolate quickly turned him into a chocolatier. Today, the Neuhaus Chocolate Shop produces more than seventy kinds of chocolate, including ultra-rich, handmade varieties and candied strips of chocolate-coated orange peel known as pailettes.

In 1896, Antoine Jacques, the man who patented the chocolate bar, founded the Jacques Chocolate Factory in the Belgian city of Eupen. Chocolatier Jacques now produces eighty tons of chocolate every day.

An eighteenth-century chateau in Chaudfontaine is one of the country's finest spas. To honor Belgium's rich chocolate tradition, the spa features a "massage au chocolat," forty-five minutes of spreadable, decadent delight.

Dear Chip

Chocolate: Here today ... Gone today!

Author Unknown

I never dreamed that one day I would have to write this letter. However, I find, for the sake of my heart, I must. To turn away from our long, satisfying relationship is the hardest thing I've ever had to do.

It's not you. You're everything a girl could ask for. You are smooth, dark, rich, and being from Switzerland only adds to your allure. Underneath your dark exterior, I have seen your soft, delicious, sometimes nutty side.

You've warmed me on cold winter nights and refreshed me on hot summer days.

I will think of you every time I drink plain milk or hot tea or eat frozen vanilla yogurt. We have shared every birthday and anniversary. How will I ever survive Valentine's Day or Easter without you?

You have to admit that in any healthy relationship, both parties should grow. However, I feel ours has been too one-sided. You have stayed the same, while I seem to have done all the growing, right out of two sizes of jeans.

The recent rise in my blood pressure and cholesterol has made me realize that I need to start over.

I would be the first to admit that our relationship has been somewhat bittersweet. This can't come as a surprise to you. I have tried to walk away before. True, in the past, I've always come back. I've never been able to make a clean break.

What makes this so difficult is knowing that no matter what I say or do, you will always take me back. All I need to do is hold out my hand.

We never pledged to be exclusive. I know that others adore you as much as I do. I must confess, I've even tried a substitute. But there is nothing like the original.

The memory of your taste will haunt me for the rest of my life.

I take all the blame. My doctor says one small dose of you each day may be beneficial to my health, but I seem to be a woman prone to excess. Your Kisses are addictive. I am never satisfied with just one.

Every day when I come home from work, I reach for you. Whenever I achieve a goal, I want to reward myself with a taste of you.

I have become obsessive. It has to stop.

You'll be happy to know that I have joined a support group. With their help and a lot of exercise, I may be able to regain my former self.

I hesitate to say good-bye.

Who knows, in a year or so, when I reach my goal, say, about 120 pounds, perhaps we will meet again. It would have to be only occasionally. We could never go back to where we are today.

I must admit that I am going to keep my intentions a

secret. This weekend I intend to indulge myself and seek
out as much of your comfort as I can.

First thing Monday morning, I will mail this letter and
start my long journey without you.

Love,
Barbara

Barbara Ann Carle

who Is Jack Canfield?

Jack Canfield is the cocreator and editor of the Chicken Soup for the Soul series, which *Time* magazine has called "the publishing phenomenon of the decade." Jack is also the coauthor of eight other bestselling books, including *The Success Principles: How to Get from Where You Are to Where You Want to Be, Dare to Win, The Aladdin Factor, You've Got to Read This Book,* and *The Power of Focus: How to Hit Your Business, Personal and Financial Targets with Absolute Certainty.*

Jack offers an online coaching program based on *The Success Principles* and offers a seven-day *Breakthrough to Success* seminar every summer, which attracts 400 people from fifteen countries around the world. Jack is the CEO of Chicken Soup for the Soul Enterprises and the Canfield Training Group in Santa Barbara, California, and founder of the Foundation for Self-Esteem in Culver City, California. He has conducted intensive personal and professional development seminars on the principles of success for over 900,000 people in twenty-one countries around the world. He has spoken to hundreds of thousands of others at numerous conferences and conventions and has been seen by millions of viewers on national television shows such as *The Today Show, Fox and Friends, Inside Edition, Hard Copy,* CNN's *Talk Back Live, 20/20, Eye to Eye,* and the NBC Nightly News and the CBS Evening News.

Jack is the recipient of many awards and honors, including three honorary doctorates and a Guinness World Records Certificate for having seven Chicken Soup for the Soul books appearing on the *New York Times* bestseller list on May 24, 1998. To write to Jack or for inquiries about Jack as a speaker, his coaching programs, or his seminars, use the following contact information:

Jack Canfield
The Canfield Companies
P.O. Box 30880 • Santa Barbara, CA 93130
phone: 805-563-2935 • fax: 805-563-2945
e-mail: info@jackcanfield.com • website: www.jackcanfield.com

who Is Mark Victor Hansen?

In the area of human potential, no one is more respected than Mark Victor Hansen. For more than thirty years, Mark has focused solely on helping people from all walks of life reshape their personal vision of what's possible. His powerful messages of possibility, opportunity, and action have created powerful change in thousands of organizations and millions of individuals worldwide.

He is a sought-after keynote speaker, bestselling author, and marketing maven. Mark is a prolific writer with many bestselling books, such as *The One Minute Millionaire, The Power of Focus, The Aladdin Factor*, and *Dare to Win*, in addition to the Chicken Soup for the Soul series. Mark is the founder of the MEGA Seminar Series. MEGA Book Marketing University and Building Your MEGA Speaking Empire are annual conferences where Mark coaches and teaches new and aspiring authors, speakers, and experts on building lucrative publishing and speaking careers. He has appeared on television (*Oprah*, CNN, and *The Today Show*), in print (*Time, U.S. News & World Report, USA Today, New York Times*, and *Entrepreneur*), and on countless radio interviews.

As a philanthropist and humanitarian, Mark works tirelessly for organizations such as Habitat for Humanity, American Red Cross, March of Dimes, Childhelp USA, and many others. He is the recipient of numerous awards that honor his entrepreneurial spirit, philanthropic heart, and business acumen. He is a lifetime member of the Horatio Alger Association of Distinguished Americans, an organization that honored Mark with the prestigious Horatio Alger Award for his extraordinary life achievements. Mark Victor Hansen is an enthusiastic crusader of what's possible and is driven to make the world a better place.

Mark Victor Hansen & Associates, Inc.
P.O. Box 7665 • Newport Beach, CA 92658
phone: 949-764-2640 • fax: 949-722-6912
website: www.markvictorhansen.com

Who Is Patricia Lorenz?

Patricia Lorenz is the coauthor of *Chicken Soup for the Chocolate Lover's Soul, Chicken Soup for the Tea Lover's Soul,* and *Chicken Soup for the Dieter's Soul, Daily Inspirations,* and she is one of the most frequent contributing writers to the Chicken Soup for the Soul series, with stories in over thirty editions.

Patricia is the author of *Life's Too Short to Fold Your Underwear, Grab the Extinguisher My Birthday Cake's On Fire, Great American Outhouse Stories, True Pilot Stories, A Hug a Day for Single Parents,* and *Stuff That Matters for Single Parents.* She has had over 400 articles published in numerous magazines and newspapers, is an award-winning newspaper columnist, and a contributing writer to seventeen Daily Guideposts books and over sixty anthologies.

As a professional speaker Patricia has entertained hundreds of groups throughout the United States with her art-of-living speeches, with topics including Humor for the Health of It, Follow Your Dreams While You're Still Awake, The Five Things We Need to Be Happy, and Learning to Love Your Struggles. She is also a sought-after speaker for women's retreats and writing conferences.

Patricia lives in Largo, Florida, where she moved after twenty-four years in Milwaukee, Wisconsin. She is the mother of four grown children and the proud grandmother of eight.

To contact Patricia about speaking engagements, visit her on the Web at www.PatriciaLorenz.com, or e-mail patricialorenz@juno.com.

contributors

Aaron Bacall's work has appeared in most national publications, several cartoon collections, and has been used for advertising, greeting cards, wall calendars and several corporate promotional books. Three of his cartoons are featured in the permanent collection at the Harvard Business School's Baker Library. He can be reached at abacall@msn.com.

Stephanie Buckwalter, an award-winning writer, has written a wide variety of material, including books for the school library market, content for websites, encyclopedia entries (somebody has to write them!), and stories about growing up in a large family. She lives in Virginia with her husband and five children.

Cheryl Butler is the patient mother of eight children under the ages of fourteen. When not sorting laundry, she writes the column "Family Zone" for magazines in southern Rhode Island and is published in *Chicken Soup For The Pre-School Mother's Soul* and *The Misadventures of Mom and Disasters of Dad.* She lives with her husband, Brian, and their fun-loving brood of five boys and three girls. Contact her at cb091987@aol.com.

Kathe Campbell lives on a western Montana mountain with her national champion mammoth donkeys, her precious Keeshond, and a few kitties. Three grown children, eleven grands, and three greats round out the herd. She has contributed to newspapers and national magazines on Alzheimer's disease, and her Montana stories are found on many e-zines. Kathe is a contributing author to the Chicken Soup for the Soul series, *People Who Make a Difference, Classic Christmas, Releasing Times, RX for Writers,* and medical journals.

Professor **Elynne Chaplik-Aleskow** is married to her best friend Richard Aleskow. She is a published writer, public speaker, and award-winning educator. The 2007 Distinguished Service Professor of Wright College in Chicago, Elynne is also the founding General Manager of WYCC-TV/Channel 20, a PBS affiliate in Chicago. Visit Elynne at www.lookaroundme.blogspot.com.

Barbara Ann Carle is a short story writer and poet. She is the mother of four and grandmother of six. Barbara is a retired police officer and resides in Friendswood, Texas, with her husband and family.

Harriet Cooper is a freelance writer living in Toronto, Canada. When not dipping into her chocolate stash, she writes about health, food, ecoproducts, family, relationships, animals, and humor. Her work has appeared in several Chicken Soup for the Soul anthologies, as well as in magazines, newsletters, newspapers, radio, and a coffee can.

Terri Duncan is a graduate of Augusta State University. She is currently a graduation coach in Evans, Georgia, and is also a devoted wife and the mother of two delightful teenagers. Her dream is to have published a full-length book suitable for children.

Christina Dymock has worked as an editor at an advertising agency and taught at the local community college. Christina makes and sells chocolate, fudge-filled Easter eggs, and after being covered in chocolate for a week, she emerges with a smile on her face. Christina currently resides in Herriman, Utah, with her husband and three energetic boys.

Susan Engebrecht moved from Colorado's Rocky Mountains to live and write under the protective shadow of Granite Peak in central Wisconsin. She is a member of Writers of

Wausau and Wisconsin Regional Writers Association. Her work has been broadcast on radio and appeared in literary publications, newspapers, and inspirational magazines.

Lori Falce is a writer and avid chocolate enthusiast. Born in Minnesota, she grew up in central Pennsylvania, where she attended Penn State. She now makes her home in Osceola Mills, Pennsylvania, with her husband, Matthew. She encourages everyone to sweeten their lives with chocolate. Lori can be reached at lorifalce@gmail.com.

Jessica R. Ferguson is a novelist, freelance writer, and coordinator for the Lamar University Write Site. Because of her husband's work, she bounces back and forth across the Texas/Louisiana line—with one fun jaunt to Scotland. Jess loves all chocolate, but especially Milk Duds.

Angela Gray is a small-town girl from Patterson, Missouri. She is a full-time secretary and illustrates children's books on the side. She has teamed up with her sister, author Jennifer Lynne Smith, on their first book, *Things I Wonder*, available online at www.hisworkpub.com. Go there to learn more about Angela!

Jean Matthew Hall lives near Charlotte, North Carolina, with her husband, Jerry. She is a retired Christian school administrator who now invests her time in their children and grandchildren, church ministries, and freelance writing. If she's going to waste calories and fat grams, they're going to be wrapped in chocolate.

Christina Hamlett is a former actress and theater director. Christina is a professional script consultant and the author of twenty-two books, 122 plays and musicals, five optioned feature films, and hundreds of articles and interviews. She and her knight-in-shining-armor husband reside in

Southern California. Visit Christina at www.absolutewrite. com/site/christina.htm.

Bonnie Compton Hanson is a chocolate lover and the author of several books for both adults and children, including the popular *Ponytail Girls* series and hundreds of published articles and poems. She also speaks for Mothers of Preschoolers (MOPS), seniors, schools, women's groups, and writing conferences. Contact Bonnie at bonnieh1@worldnet.att.net.

Patrick Hardin is a freelance cartoonist whose work appears in a variety of periodicals and books around the world. Patrick can be reached at hardin_cartoons@comcast.net.

Sydney Salter Husseman lives in Utah with her husband, two daughters, two cats, and two oversized dogs. She has written stories for *Appleseeds, Children's Playmate, FACES, Hopscotch, Story Friends, Wee Ones* magazine, and Blooming Tree Press's *Summer Shorts* anthology. She loves reading, writing, traveling, and exceptional chocolate (well, sometimes *any* chocolate will do).

Jennie Ivey lives in Cookeville, Tennessee. She is a newspaper columnist and author of two books, *Tennessee Tales the Textbooks Don't Tell* and *E Is for Elvis*. She has published numerous fiction and nonfiction pieces, including stories in five Chicken Soup for the Soul collections. Jennie can be reached at jivey@frontiernet.net.

Patricia Carroll Johnson is a freelance writer and works full time as a special features editor with three newspapers. She is the mother of three and grandmother of eight. She enjoys reading, knitting, spinning, and weaving, and never misses an opportunity to eat chocolate or go to the library.

Ruth Jones worked in organizational development for over twenty-five years until she gave up her consulting practice and started writing. She has completed the very rough draft of her first novel and has plans for a second one. Ruth lives in Tennessee with her husband, Terry.

Elizabeth Kann coauthored the children's book *Pinkalicious* (HarperCollins) with her sister, which they adapted into "Pinkalicious the Musical." She is a doctor who lives in Pennsylvania with her husband and three children. Her essays have appeared in *Chicken Soup for the New Mom's Soul* and elsewhere. Visit Elizabeth at www.elizabethkann. com.

Nancy Julien Kopp has published stories, articles, essays, children's stories, and poetry in magazines, newspapers, e-zines, and anthologies, including *Chicken Soup for the Father and Daughter Soul, Chicken Soup for the Sister's Soul 2,* and *Chicken Soup for the Dieter's Soul.* She is a former teacher and still enjoys teaching through the written word.

Robyn Kurth is a freelance writer with over fifteen years of experience writing and producing corporate and industrial videos and a specialty in "writing for the ear." A native of the Chicago area, she currently resides in Orlando, Florida, with her husband, Greg, and children, Alex and Zell. Robyn can be reached at rwordworks@earth link.net.

John J. Lesjack, a graduate of both East Detroit High School and San Francisco State University, is a retired teacher who is into his second career of writing and speaking. His work has appeared in *Science of Mind* magazine, *Grit* magazine, *Whispers from Heaven,* and other national publications. He has three children, none of whom like chocolate. John can be reached at lesjack@gmail.com.

Rhonda C. Leverett continues to enjoy chocolate therapy with her family in The Woodlands, Texas. She also contributes to *The Write Ingredients Newsletter,* sometimes wins writing contests, and is at work on her first book, a bitter-sweet, coming-of-age memoir set in the seventies. Visit Rhonda at www.leverett.com.

J. M. Long lives in Florida. Her writing has been published in various print media, as well as broadcast on television. This is her first piece for Chicken Soup for the Soul.

Loree Lough is a bestselling author whose stories have earned numerous awards. Loree teaches writing and frequently shares industry insights with audiences in the U.S. and abroad. She and her sweeter-than-chocolate husband live in Maryland with a formerly abused, now-spoiled Pointer. Visit Loree at www.loreelough.com.

Gary Luerding resides in southern Oregon with Lynne, his wife of forty-four years. He is a frequent Chicken Soup for the Soul contributor and author of "The Sunny Side" appearing in *Cup of Comfort for Mothers and Sons,* and *Inshore Ocean Fishing for Dummies.* Gary can be reached at garyluer@frontiernet.net.

Lynne MacKnight is the author of *Celebration of Motherhood with Love & Laughter,* a collection of essays. Her work has also appeared in the *New York Times,* the *Times,* and the *Sandpaper.* She is the mother of three grown children and grandmother of five.

L. J. Martin lives with her husband and two chocoholic sons in the Valley of the Sun. They are all looking forward to celebrating Grandma Marie's ninetieth birthday on a dinner cruise along the Illinois River. And yes, there will be lots of chocolate cake.

Sandy McKeown is a mother of five, grandmother of two, and Mentor of Many (M.O.M.). She is a contributing author to *Laundry Tales to Lighten Your Load* and *One Year Life Verse Devotional.* In addition she speaks nationally with Celebrate

Moms.org. She and her husband teach premarriage sessions and mentor those discovering the challenges of rearing children while keeping their marriages strong. Visit Sandy at www.sandymckeown.com.

Michelle McLean is a fledgling novelist and freelance writer. She has a master's degree in English, and her essays have been published on several online sites and in two previous Chicken Soup for the Soul books. She is currently enjoying time at home with her children while finishing work on her first novel.

Bill Meissner is the author of six books, including the short story collections *Hitting into the Wind* (Random House/SMU Press, paperback) and *The Road to Cosmos* (University of Notre Dame Press). His stories and articles have appeared in *Minnesota Monthly, Minneapolis/St. Paul Magazine, Lake Country Journal,* and various Sunday picture magazines, including the *Miami Herald* and the *Oregonian*. He is the Director of Creative Writing at St. Cloud State University in Minnesota.

Peggy Morris is a chocoholic, freelance writer, pastor's wife, and mother of two amazing sons. Her inspiring words can be found on greeting cards by DaySpring, Gallant Greetings, Christian Inspiration and in *Woman's World* magazine. You can contact Peggy at peggymorris@htcog.net.

Amy Mullis lives in upstate South Carolina with husband, Bill, and teenage sons, Ryan and Jeffrey. She works part time as a church secretary to support her hot chocolate habit. Amy's work has also been published in *Chicken Soup for the Beach Lover's Soul.*

Linda Newton is a graduate of Azusa Pacific University. Linda works on the counseling staff at Sierra Pines Church in Oakhurst, California. A mother of three grown children, she has learned there is nothing that can't be conquered with Kleenex and a box of chocolates. She is represented nationally as a speaker for CLASServices and is regularly invited to speak at retreats, conferences, and seminars. Visit Linda at www.lindanewtonspeaks.com.

Linda O'Connell, a veteran early childhood educator in St. Louis, Missouri, teaches a senior citizen writing class. She believes that this world would be better if there were more humor and laughter. Her favorite pastimes are walking the beach with her husband and writing. Their grandchildren provide many "laugh lines."

Dorri Olds, a native New Yorker, earned a B.F.A. in 1985 and has been a graphic designer ever since. In 1994 she started her Manhattan-based business, DorriOlds.com. Her short stories have been published in two Chicken Soup for the Soul books, in *New Woman* magazine, and in the book *At Grandmother's Table.*

Barbara Paulson lives in northeast Ohio. Her recently published book, *No Going Back,* is historical fiction coauthored with Norah Griggs. Her poetry appears in *Rocklady: The Building of a Labyrinth.* Visit Barbara at www.rocklady.ws.

Linda Kaullen Perkins' short stories, articles, and essays have appeared in various publications, including *The Rocking Chair Reader* series and *A Cup of Comfort for Weddings* by Adams Media. Author of over ninety-five published stories, Linda is a member of Romance Writers of America and the Missouri Writers' Guild. Visit Linda at http://hometown.aol.com/squatters5/lindakaullenperkins.html.

Stephanie Piro is one of King Features' team of women cartoonists and is the Saturday chick in "Six Chix." Stephanie's line of gift items available from her company, Strip T's, can be seen on www.stephaniepiro.com, and her new book, *My Cat Loves Me Naked*, is available at bookstores everywhere. Contact Stephanie by e-mailing stephaniepiro@verizon.net, or writing 27 River Road, Farmington, NH 03835.

Helen Kay Polaski is a freelance writer and book editor. Her most recent projects include compiling and editing *A Cup of Comfort for Weddings* and *Classic Christmas: True Stories of Holiday Cheer* and *Goodwill.* Helen can be reached at hkpolaski@yahoo. com.

Felice Prager is a professional freelance writer from Scottsdale, Arizona, with local, national, and international writing credits. In addition to writing, Felice is an multisensory educational therapist, which is a fancy way of saying she works with children and adults who have moderate to severe learning disabilities.

Bruce Robinson is an award-winning, internationally published cartoonist whose work has appeared in numerous consumer and trade periodicals including the *National Enquirer, The Saturday Evening Post, Woman's World, The Sun, First, Highlights for Children,* and more. He is also author of the cartoon book, *Good Medicine.* E-mail him at cartoonsbybruce robinson@hotmail.com.

Sallie Rodman's writing has appeared in various Chicken Soup for the Soul anthologies and on bags of Chicken Soup dog food. Her articles are in *Byline, Romantic Homes, Mystery Review,* and *Angels on Earth.* Whether it's Kisses, bars, turtles, malted milk balls, or truffles, Sallie is a confirmed chocoholic and chooses not to be cured. Sallie can be reached at sa.rodman@verizon.net.

Merrie Root is a mom and grandma who enjoys her family above all else. Merrie is published in *God Allows U-Turns 2* and several other anthologies. Her poetry earned her a silver medal from the International Library of Poetry.

Bill Satterlee is a retired supermarket firm vice president. His writing experience includes company training manuals and policy and procedure documentation. Many of his articles dealing with history, family remembrances, and life experiences are posted on several Internet sites and have been published in the local newspaper.

Darcy Silvers is a freelance writer in the Philadelphia area who enjoys writing about chocolate almost as much as she does eating it. Her dream job would be working in a chocolate candy factory, as in the famous *I Love Lucy* episode

Jean Stewart is a chocolate-loving writer in Mission Viejo, California, who has graced her twin daughters, and is still sharing with her husband of forty-six years, the joys of dark chocolate. Her family, parenting, and travel stories can be found in other Chicken Soup for the Soul books, as well as newspapers and magazines.

Radhika Basu Thakur has a degree in English Literature from Calcutta University and holds a diploma in journalism and newswriting from the London School of Journalism. She has written and edited content for various websites and for the popular news daily *The Telegraph*. Radhika is pursuing a postgraduate degree in arts and media at Griffith University in Australia. Read Radhika's blog at http://life-and-all-that-jazz.blogspot.com.

Cristy Trandahl is a freelance writer and mother of six. She contributes to many nationally distributed anthologies and speaks on parenting issues. For more info and support for chocolate addiction, visit Cristy at www.cristytrandahl.com.

Joyce Tres is a writer living in California. Her short stories, essays, poetry, and articles have appeared in various publications. Joyce recently finished her first novel. Visit Joyce at http://joycetres.net.

Samantha Ducloux Waltz is a freelance writer in Portland, Oregon. Her personal essays are her favorite way to sort out her always interesting, often chaotic world, and can be seen in a number of current anthologies and the *Christian Science Monitor.*

Permissions

We would like to acknowledge the many publishers and individuals who granted us permission to reprint the cited material. Any content not specifically attributed to an author was written by Patricia Lorenz. The stories that were penned anonymously, that are in the public domain, or that were written by Jack Canfield, Mark Victor Hansen, or Patricia Lorenz are not included in this listing.

Fifteen-Cent Surprise. Reprinted by permission of Jean Matthew Hall. ©2006 Jean Matthew Hall.

Skinny Dotty and Her Chocolates. Reprinted by permission of Dorri Olds. ©2006 Dorri Olds.

Cards and Kisses. Reprinted by permission of Linda Newton. ©2007 Linda Newton.

Full Confession. Reprinted by permission of Cheryl L. Butler. ©2006 Cheryl L. Butler.

A Guy Speaks Out for Chocolate. Reprinted by permission of Bill Meissner. ©2007 Bill Meissner.

Chocolate-Covered Cherries. Reprinted by permission of John J. Lesjack. ©2006 John J. Lesjack.

Oh, Fudge! Reprinted by permission of Bonnie Compton Hanson. ©2006 Bonnie Compton Hanson.

Sweet Chocolate Sunshine. Reprinted by permission of Radhika Basu Thakur. ©2006 Radhika Basu Thakur.

Bittersweet Birthday. Reprinted by permission of Cristy L. Trandahl. ©2006 Cristy L. Trandahl.

A Nickel and Chocolate Cake with Candy-Bar Icing. Reprinted by permission of Bill Satterlee. ©1996 Bill Satterlee.

Sweet Shoppe. Reprinted by permission of Patricia Carroll Johnson. ©2006 Patricia Carroll Johnson. Originally published in *Chicken Soup for the Shopper's Soul.*

A Good Chocolate Is Hard to Find. Reprinted by permission of Robyn Kurth. ©2006 Robyn Kurth.

Love at First Truffle. Reprinted by permission of Christina Hamlett. ©2007 Christina Hamlett.

Chocolate Attack. Reprinted by permission of Lynne MacKnight. ©2000 Lynne

MacKnight. Originally appeared in *Celebration of Motherhood with Love and Laughter.*

A Taste of Chocolate. Reprinted by permission of Gary B. Luerding. ©2006 Gary B. Luerding.

Some Like It Hot. Reprinted by permission of Amy Mullis. ©2006 Amy Mullis.

Chocolate Milk and Bologna. Reprinted by permission of Stephanie Buckwalter. ©2007 Stephanie Buckwalter.

Candy Kisses. Reprinted by permission of Kathe Campbell. ©2007 Kathe Campbell.

Say It with Chocolate. Reprinted by permission of Michelle McLean. ©2007 Michelle McLean.

Finger-Lickin' Good! Reprinted by permission of Victoria J. Hanson. ©2006 Victoria J. Hanson.

Chocolate Shake and Chocolate Cake. Reprinted by permission of Joyce P. Tres. ©2006 Joyce P. Tres.

Chocolate Bunnies. Reprinted by permission of Linda Kaullen Perkins. ©2007 Linda Kaullen Perkins.

A Spoonful of Fudge. Reprinted by permission of Nancy Julien Kopp. ©2006 Nancy Julien Kopp.

The Chocoholic Grandma. Reprinted by permission of L. J. Martin. ©2006 L. J. Martin.

Somebody's Sweetheart. Reprinted by permission of Linda Newton. ©2007 Linda Newton.

Accomplices in Chocolate. Reprinted by permission of Barbara Paulson. ©2007 Barbara Paulson.

In Emergency, Break Glass. Reprinted by permission of Sandy McKeown. ©2006 Sandy McKeown.

A Lifelong Love of Chocolate. Reprinted by permission of Darcy Silvers. ©2007 Darcy Silvers.

The Chocolate Marauder. Reprinted by permission of Terri Duncan. ©2007 Terri Duncan.

The Revolving Door. Reprinted by permission of Elynne Chaplik-Aleskow. ©2006 Elynne Chaplik-Aleskow.

Wanted: A Cold Day in Florida. Reprinted by permission of J. M. Long. ©2007 J. M. Long.

Just Like Grandma's. Reprinted by permission of Susan Engebrecht. ©2007 Susan Engebrecht.

Chester and the Chocolate-Covered Cherries. Reprinted by permission of Jean Stewart. ©2006 Jean Stewart.

Sharing Chocolate. Reprinted by permission of Samantha Ducloux Waltz. ©2007 Samantha Ducloux Waltz.

A Chocolate Tradition. Reprinted by permission of Christina Dymock. ©2006 Christina Dymock.

The Gift of Chocolate and Love. Reprinted by permission of Merrie Root. ©2006 Merrie Root.

Chocolate—Eat Your Heart Out. Reprinted by permission of Harriet Cooper. ©2006 Harriet Cooper.

Is There Chocolate in Heaven? Reprinted by permission of Loree Lough. ©2007 Loree Lough.

Auntie Yum. Reprinted by permission of Sydney Salter Husseman. ©2007 Sydney Salter Husseman.

A Fudgeless Fridge. Reprinted by permission of Elizabeth Kann. ©2001 Elizabeth Kann. Originally appeared in the *Pittsburgh Post Gazette.*

House of Chocolate. Reprinted by permission of Helen Kay Polaski. ©2006 Helen Kay Polaski.

Kisses for Daddy. Reprinted by permission of Peggy Morris. ©2007 Peggy Morris.

Sharing Secret Indulgences. Reprinted by permission of Felice Prager. ©2004 Felice Prager.

The Secret Ingredient. Reprinted by permission of Ruth Jones. ©2006 Ruth Jones.

The Dud in White. Reprinted by permission of Jessica R. Ferguson. ©2007 Jessica R. Ferguson.

It Turns to Love. Reprinted by permission of Rhonda C. Leverett. ©2007 Rhonda C. Leverett.

Thank You, Santa. Reprinted by permission of Jennie Ivey. ©2007 Jennie Ivey.

The Old Red Devil. Reprinted by permission of Lori Falce. ©2007 Lori Falce.

The Game Plan. Reprinted by permission of Sallie A. Rodman. ©2007 Sallie A. Rodman.

Heavenly Cookies. Reprinted by permission of Linda O'Connell. ©2006 Linda O'Connell.

The Way Home. Reprinted by permission of Angela Gray. ©2007 Angela Gray.

Dear Chip. Reprinted by permission of Barbara Ann Carle. ©2007 Barbara Ann Carle.

Chicken Soup for the Soul

www.chickensoup.com